ROSARY MEDITATIONS
DEEPENING AND ENRICHING
A REMARKABLE PRAYER

Rosary Meditations

Deepening and Enriching a Remarkable Prayer

Amy Troolin

Copyright © 2014 by Amy Troolin

ISBN-13: 978-1494354893
ISBN-10: 1494354896

Scripture taken from the New Revised Standard Version Bible: Catholic Edition, copyright 1989, 1993, Division of Christian Education of the National Council of the Churches of Christ in the United States of America. Used by permission. All rights reserved.

For my parents with much love.

Contents

Introduction 1

Joyful Mysteries
The Annunciation 5
The Visitation 13
The Nativity 21
The Presentation of Jesus in the Temple 31
The Finding of Jesus in the Temple 41

Luminous Mysteries
The Baptism of Jesus 51
The Wedding at Cana 61
The Proclamation of the Kingdom and the Call to Conversion 71
The Transfiguration 83
The Institution of the Eucharist 93

Sorrowful Mysteries
The Agony in the Garden 103
The Scourging at the Pillar 117
The Crowning of Thorns 125
The Carrying of the Cross 133
The Crucifixion 143

Glorious Mysteries
The Resurrection 155

The Ascension	169
The Descent of the Holy Spirit	177
The Assumption	189
The Coronation of Our Blessed Mother in Heaven	197
Notes	205

Introduction

Have you ever sat down to pray the Rosary only to find that your mind drifts off in all directions and stubbornly refuses to come back to the mystery at hand? Don't feel bad! This is a common problem even for those who have made a firm commitment to pray the Rosary frequently and devoutly.

There are countless sets of Rosary meditations available online and in books and booklets that are designed to help you stay focused on your meditation. Many of these have proven to be quite helpful in my own prayer life. So why am I offering yet another set of Rosary meditations? How is this series different from those already available?

Many, even most, Rosary meditations are relatively short. They are designed to be read just before each decade or Hail Mary, and they focus on only one or two aspects of each mystery. While these brief commentaries can and do stimulate meditation, they can also become a little worn out over time because they lack depth.

The Rosary meditations you will find in this book are different. First, they are longer and more detailed than most meditations. Second, they provide a wealth of information about each mystery. Third, they are designed as a reference to be read before beginning the Rosary and then consulted as necessary during the prayer to stimulate meditation and curb mind-wandering. Fourth,

Rosary Meditations

they can be used almost indefinitely because they offer so many options for profitable reflection.

Each meditation is organized in six sections:

1. Scripture References – I have listed the primary Scriptural text or texts for each Rosary mystery. Sometimes I like to pray the Rosary with the Bible open on my lap. I read portions of the text as I pray, meditating on the Scriptures and allowing the Word of God to speak to me directly.

2. The Story in Brief – Telling yourself the story of each mystery during the Rosary can sometimes stimulate fruitful meditation. As you recount the mystery, in my words or your own, you might find that one aspect or another will strike you and lead you into an intimate conversation with God.

3. Points to Ponder – Each point to ponder invites you to delve deeply into the mystery and explore its details and layers of meaning. I will give you enough information to get started; then you can take it from there and let God lead you into your own personalized meditation. Do not be afraid to get creative. God gave you your intellect and imagination for a reason. Use them well!

4. Application Questions – An important aspect of meditation involves applying the mysteries of the Rosary to your own life and examining what God is trying to say to you personally. I will present some questions. Your job is to answer them honestly.

5. Prayer, Prayer, and More Prayer – The Rosary is a prayer that stimulates more prayer, endless prayer, if you open your heart and mind to God. The *Catechism of the*

Introduction

Catholic Church (#2626-2649) identifies five different forms of prayer: blessing and adoration, praise, thanksgiving, intercession, and petition. I will offer a suggestion for further prayer in each of these forms. Feel free to compose your own prayers as the Holy Spirit leads you. You might even try to focus your entire meditation on a particular prayer form. I periodically pray an intercessory Rosary during which I lift up individuals or various groups of people for each mystery. For example, during the Joyful Mystery of the Nativity, I pray for women who are about to give birth and for newborns. There are endless possibilities.

6. Quotes from the Saints – In the final section of each meditation, I offer several quotes from the saints. These quotes have plenty of depth to them, and you might find yourself concentrating on a single quote for an entire decade. Most of the quotes come from St. Thomas Aquinas' *Catena Aurea*, which is a collection of commentaries on the Gospels from the Fathers of the Church. Others are drawn from various collections of saints' writings and quotations. Please see the endnotes for full source citations.

As you prepare to pray the Rosary, you can choose to focus on any of these sections, but please do not try to meditate on too much at once. One or two points to ponder; a point to ponder and an application question; or one quote from a saint, for example, should be plenty for each mystery. You probably already know that ten Hail Marys can fly by very quickly if you are in the midst of a good meditation. The meditations in this book should supply enough material for fruitful reflection to last a long, long time.

Rosary Meditations

By this point you might be asking, "Where is all this coming from?" I have been praying the Rosary daily for over ten years, and even though my mind wanders frequently, God has led me into some beautiful meditations that have drawn me closer to Him. Much of the material in this book comes out of my own prayer and study. I have found it valuable in my spiritual life, and I want to share it with as many people as possible.

I hope and pray that these meditations will help you as you seek to enrich your Rosary prayer and meditation, curb distractions, and most importantly, grow closer to God.

A book like this one is never written in isolation. I would like, first and foremost, to thank my mother, LaJune Troolin, for her unending patience and support, her excellent ideas, and her top-notch proofreading skills. I would also like to thank my best friend, T.J. Duchene, for his help with formatting the manuscript and solving a whole bevy of computer problems.

Finally, I offer thanks and praise to our Lord Jesus Christ, and through Him, to the Almighty Father and the Holy Spirit, Blessed Trinity, Three in One. You are my Savior and my God, my Jesus, and I love You. Amen.

The First Joyful Mystery: The Annunciation

Scripture References

Luke 1:26-38; Isaiah 7:14

The Story in Brief

Mary was a young, but very holy, girl from the town of Nazareth in Galilee. Her neighbors probably never realized how holy she really was. They certainly did not understand her destiny. One day, the archangel Gabriel appeared to Mary. She was perplexed at his greeting, but he told her not to be afraid, for she was filled with grace, and the Lord was with her. He announced that she would bear a Son named Jesus, a Son Who would be the Son of the Most High God and would reign over an unending Kingdom from the throne of David. Mary asked how this could be since she was a virgin. The angel had a ready answer. The Holy Spirit would come upon Mary, and the "power of the Most High" would overshadow her. Her Child would be holy. Nothing was impossible for God, the angel concluded, for Mary's relative Elizabeth had conceived a child in her old age. After hearing all this, Mary said, "Here am I, the servant of the Lord; let it be with me according to your word." She gave herself fully to God and offered her entire life to the fulfillment of His plan.

Rosary Meditations

Points to Ponder

1. Nazareth in Galilee was an out-of-the-way spot, and no one expected it to be so important in the life of the Messiah. It has, however, a suggestive name. Nazareth means "branch" or "watch, guard, or keep."[1] Meditate on the significance of Nazareth, especially its supposed unimportance and its symbolic name.

2. What was Mary doing when the angel appeared to her? I like to think that she was totally immersed in prayer. Imagine Mary at prayer. How would she have spoken to God? What kind of relationship did she have with God?

3. The angel's greeting to Mary was literally "Hail, you who have been fully graced." What does it mean to have been fully graced? Catholics believe that Mary was immaculately conceived, that is, conceived without sin, in preparation for her motherhood. Reflect on Mary's Immaculate Conception.

4. The angel told Mary, "The Lord is with you." Ponder how God is with all of us in an intimate way.

5. Consider Mary's reaction to the angel's greeting. Was she afraid, perplexed, pondering, wondering, or some combination of all of these?

6. The angel told Mary that she had "found favor" with God. Meditate on these reassuring words. What did Mary think when she heard them?

7. The angel told Mary that she would be overshadowed by the power of the Holy Spirit. Read Genesis 1:1-2. How are the words similar to the angel's message? Could the

The Annunciation

angel have been announcing the arrival of a new creation? Meditate on this new creation.

8. With the Annunciation, the promise of Isaiah 7:14 was fulfilled. Read Isaiah 7:14, and ponder God's promises and their fulfillment.

9. The Gospel places great emphasis on Mary's virginity. Jesus' conception was truly miraculous. Think deeply about this miracle.

10. Did Mary fully understand what the angel was telling her? Did she know Who her Son would be? Because she was conceived without sin, Mary retained the gift of preternatural knowledge, the kind of knowledge Adam and Eve would have had before the Fall, a type of knowledge infused directly by God.[2] Mary, then, may have understood that she was being chosen as the mother of the Messiah and even as the mother of God. Reflect on this knowledge. How did it influence Mary's decision to accept her role?

11. The angel used several descriptive words and titles for Jesus: great, Son of the Most High, holy, Son of God, and King ruling on the throne of David. Ponder each of these words and titles. What do they tell us about Jesus and His mission?

12. Contrast Mary's question "How can this be?" with Zechariah's question a few verses earlier: "How will I know that this is so?" Mary was not focusing on herself. She believed what the angel told her, but she wanted to know the details of God's wonderful plan. Many saints and theologians claim that Mary had made a vow of virginity prior to the Annunciation. Mary trusted that

Rosary Meditations

God would not compromise her vow, but she wanted to know how. Reflect on Mary's question and her reasons for asking it.

13. The angel told Mary that nothing would be impossible with God. What a marvelous reassurance! What does it mean that nothing will be impossible with God?

14. The angel waited for Mary's answer, and Mary was free to say "yes" or "no" as she willed. Ponder God's amazing respect for human freedom.

15. Mary surrendered herself totally to God and to His plan. She humbly called herself His servant or handmaid. Meditate on what it means to be a servant of God who surrenders completely to Him.

16. When the angel told Mary that her Son would reign forever, he offered a great promise, provided hope for the whole world, and foretold a new Kingdom. Reflect on Jesus' reign.

17. The angel gave Mary a sign of God's power when he told her about Elizabeth's pregnancy. Why did he do that?

18. The Son of God became incarnate as a small embryo in His mother's womb. Ponder this awesome mystery.

Application Questions

1. Does God send messengers to you? What kinds of messengers? How do you listen and respond? How might you open your heart and your mind to hear God more clearly?

The Annunciation

2. What is your response when you do not understand the messages God sends you? Are you perplexed or frightened or both?

3. What is your prayer life like? Are you ever totally immersed in prayer? How might you become more attentive and devoted in prayer?

4. How much do you value chastity in your life?

5. How is the Holy Spirit at work in you and in your circumstances?

6. Are you comfortable enough with God to ask Him questions? Do you believe that He will answer? Do you listen closely for His response? How might you improve your listening skills?

7. Are you a faithful servant of the Lord? Why or why not? In what ways can you grow in faithfulness and service to God?

8. Are there any areas of your life in which God is waiting for your "yes"? What is holding you back from giving Him that "yes"?

Prayer, Prayer, and More Prayer

Blessing and Adoration – The Word became Man and dwelt among us. Lord, we bless You because in Your greatness You descended to our world and took on our human weakness in everything except sin. We bow our heads in humble silence before You. Please fill our hearts with Your love.

Rosary Meditations

Praise – We praise You, Lord, because You came to save us. You are so powerful, yet You became a small embryo in Your mother's womb because You love us that much. You are awesome, God, in the truest sense of the word.

Thanksgiving – We thank You, Lord, for coming among us as a human being. We thank You for loving us so much that You became the weakest and most dependent of beings so that one day You might give us an intimate share in divine life.

Intercession – We lift up to You in prayer, Lord, all those who find themselves in difficult situations, all those who are struggling to say "yes" to God in their lives, and all those who are being called by God for a special vocation.

Petition – Open our hearts, Lord, to Your message for our lives and give us the courage to say "yes" to You and to be Your faithful servants.

Quotes from the Saints

"To the virgin Mary was sent, not any one of the angels, but the archangel Gabriel; for upon this service it was meet that the highest angel should come, as being the bearer of the highest of all tidings. He is therefore marked by a particular name, to signify what was his effectual part in the work. For Gabriel is interpreted, 'the strength of God.' By the strength of God then was He to be announced Who was coming as the God of strength, and mighty in battle, to put down the powers of the air." - St. Gregory the Great

"And it is well said, *Full of grace*, for to others, grace comes in part; into Mary at once the fullness of grace

The Annunciation

wholly infused itself. She truly is full of grace through whom has been poured forth upon every creature the abundant rain of the Holy Spirit. But already He was with the Virgin Who sent the angel to the Virgin. The Lord preceded His messenger, for He could not be confined by place Who dwells in all places. Whence it follows, *The Lord is with you.*" - St. Jerome

"She wondered also at the new form of blessing, unheard of before, reserved for Mary alone." - St. Ambrose

"But he who earns favor in the sight of God has nothing to fear. Hence it follows, *For you have found favor before God*. But how shall anyone find it, except through the means of his humility. For God gives grace to the humble." - St. John Chrysostom

"It was Mary's part neither to refuse belief in the Angel, nor too hastily take to herself the divine message. How subdued her answer is, compared with the words of the Priest [Zechariah]. Then said Mary to the Angel, *How shall this be?* She says, *How shall this be?* He answers, *Whereby shall I know this?* He refuses to believe that which he says he does not know, and seeks as it were still further authority for belief. She avows herself willing to do that which she doubts not will be done, but how, she is anxious to know. Mary had read, *Behold, she shall conceive and bear a son*. She believed therefore that it should be but how it was to take place she had never read, for even to so great a prophet this had not been revealed. So great a mystery was not to be divulged by the mouth of man, but of an Angel." - St. Ambrose

"Behold now the humility, the devotion of the virgin. For it follows, *But Mary said, Behold the handmaid of the*

Lord. She calls herself His handmaid, who is chosen to be His mother, so far was she from being exalted by the sudden promise. At the same time also by calling herself handmaid, she claimed to herself in no other way the prerogative of such great grace than that she might do what was commanded her. For about to bring forth One meek and lowly, she was bound herself to show forth lowliness. As it follows, *Be it to me according to your word*. You have her submission, you see her wish. *Behold the handmaid of the Lord*, signifies the readiness of duty. *Be it to me according to your word*, the conception of the wish." - St. Ambrose[3]

The Second Joyful Mystery: The Visitation

Scripture References

Luke 1:39-56; 1 Samuel 2:1-10; Genesis 18:1-15

The Story in Brief

The archangel Gabriel had told Mary that her relative Elizabeth was expecting a baby even though Elizabeth was beyond child-bearing age. Mary set out almost immediately for the hill county of Judea where Elizabeth lived with her husband, Zechariah. When Elizabeth heard Mary's joyful greeting, she felt the baby leap in her womb and found herself filled with the Holy Spirit. She cried out in a loud voice, blessing Mary and the Infant in Mary's womb. In response, Mary proclaimed her "Magnificat," a song of praise to God for the mercies He was showing to Israel and to the whole world. Mary stayed with Elizabeth for three months before returning home to Nazareth.

Points to Ponder

1. Judea was a long way from Nazareth, and travel in those days was anything but easy. Meditate on Mary's journey. How and with whom did she travel? What risks did she take? What kinds of hardship did she suffer? How did she respond to inconveniences and even danger?

Rosary Meditations

2. The archangel never told Mary to visit Elizabeth, but Mary went anyway with haste. She sacrificed herself and her desires, accepted the role of a servant, and offered an immediate response to an order not explicitly given. Ponder Mary's servanthood.

3. Mary acted out of pure love. Reflect on that love.

4. Mary was not undertaking her long journey to verify that the archangel's words were true. If she had been so motivated, she would have visited Elizabeth before saying yes to God's request. Mary trusted God to tell her the truth and to guide her life with love. Think about Mary's deep trust in God.

5. Mary went in haste. Why did she depart so quickly?

6. When Mary arrived at Elizabeth and Zechariah's home, the baby John was filled with the Holy Spirit, causing him to leap for joy in his mother's womb. The Spirit also filled Elizabeth with knowledge and awe. Meditate on the Holy Spirit's marvelous activity.

7. Elizabeth cried out in a loud voice. She spoke prophetic words that described and praised what God was doing in the world. Try to grasp Elizabeth's mental and spiritual state at this climatic moment.

8. Elizabeth called Mary blessed for two reasons: her motherhood and her faith. Ponder these blessings.

9. Reflect on the humility of Mary and Elizabeth.

The Visitation

10. This mystery offers a strong argument against abortion, for we observe the presence and action of two unborn children. Ponder this argument.

11. What does it mean to magnify the Lord? Mary is like a magnifying glass. She is transparent, but she makes the Lord appear larger to those who look at Him through her. Meditate on this important role of Mary.

12. We have the duty to call Mary blessed. We must not ignore her or deprive her of her rightful place in God's plan. Instead, we should venerate her, for the Holy Spirit, Who spoke through her, said that all generations would call her blessed. What is true devotion to Mary?

13. How did Mary emphasize God's work in her life and God's mercy in the lives of all people?

14. What does it mean to scatter the proud in the thoughts of their hearts?

15. God's activity is often unexpected and tends to be the opposite of human norms and standards. For example, He casts people down so that He may lift them up. Think closely about this reality. What does it tell us about our priorities in life?

16. Mary recognized her role in salvation history and proclaimed that a prophecy had been fulfilled. Ponder Mary's role and the fulfillment of prophecy.

17. Reflect on Mary and Elizabeth's spiritual friendship. What did they do and talk about during the three months they spent together?

Rosary Meditations

18. Read 1 Samuel 2:1-10, and ponder the parallels between Mary and Hannah. Read Genesis 18:1-15, and ponder the parallels between Elizabeth and Sarah.

<u>Application Questions</u>

1. How quickly do you respond when you notice God prompting you to act with love?

2. What are your motives for doing good to other people? Are they pure, filled with self-interest, or mixed?

3. What is your attitude toward serving others?

4. How is the Holy Spirit moving and working in you? How are you responding?

5. How do you honor Mary? What is your attitude toward her? Do you recognize her for who she is and treat her accordingly?

6. Do you believe what has been spoken to you by the Lord?

7. How can you magnify the Lord?

8. How much time do you spend rejoicing in the Lord?

9. Are you a humble person? Why or why not?

10. How much do you trust in God's mercy?

11. What great things has God done for you? How is He working in your life?

The Visitation

12. How are you being called to counter the norms and standards of the world?

13. Do you believe that God fulfills His promises? Why or why not?

14. Have you formed any close, spiritual friendships? How might you cultivate those you have and develop more?

Prayer, Prayer, and More Prayer

Blessing and Adoration – Dearest Lord, we bless You for sending the Holy Spirit upon Mary and Elizabeth. We bow our heads in silent adoration as we wait for Your Holy Spirit to fill us and teach us to speak and pray according to Your will.

Praise – Jesus, we praise You! Even as a tiny infant in Your mother's womb, Your presence sanctified John the Baptist, who was still in his mother's womb. What amazing power and love You have poured out upon Your people over the centuries and still lavish on us today!

Thanksgiving – We thank You, Lord Jesus, for Your mother, who is our mother, too. We thank You for the gift of the Holy Spirit. We thank You for doing such great things for us and for having mercy on us. We thank You for lifting up the lowly and filling the hungry with good things. We thank You for keeping the promise You made centuries ago and coming to live among us as a Man to save us and open the gates of Heaven for us.

Intercession – Lord, we lift up to You all mothers-to-be and their babies. We ask You to bless them and keep

Rosary Meditations

them safe and healthy. We also lift up to You all travelers, Lord. Guide them and guard them on their journeys.

Petition – Lord, we beg You, make us lowly and humble before You. Allow our souls to magnify You. Have mercy on us, Lord, and fill us with good things, for we are hungry for You and for Your love.

Quotes from the Saints

"But soon the blessed fruits of Mary's coming and our Lord's presence are made evident. For it follows, *And it came to pass, that when Elisabeth heard the salutation of Mary, the babe leaped in her womb.* Mark the distinction and propriety of each word. Elisabeth first heard the word, but John first experienced the grace. She heard by the order of nature, he leaped by reason of the mystery. She perceived the coming of Mary, he the coming of the Lord." - St. Ambrose

"[Elizabeth] was touched with the spirit of prophecy at once, both as to the past, present, and future. She knew that Mary had believed the promises of the Angel; she perceived when she gave her the name of mother, that Mary was carrying in her womb the Redeemer of mankind; and when she foretold that all things would be accomplished, she saw also what was to follow in the future." - St. Gregory the Great

"The first-fruit of the Spirit is peace and joy. Because then the holy Virgin had drunk in all the graces of the Spirit, she rightly adds, *And my spirit has leaped for joy.* She means the same thing, soul and spirit. But the frequent mention of leaping for joy in the Scriptures implies a certain bright and cheerful state of mind in those who are

The Visitation

worthy. Hence the Virgin exults in the Lord with an unspeakable springing (and bounding) of the heart for joy, and in the breaking forth into utterance of a noble affection it follows, *in God my Savior*." - St. Basil

Rosary Meditations

The Third Joyful Mystery: The Nativity

Scripture References

Luke 2:1-20; Matthew 1:18-2:19; Isaiah 7:14; Isaiah 11:1-5; Micah 5:2-5

The Story in Brief

Sometime after Mary returned from her visit to Elizabeth, Joseph discovered that his betrothed was expecting a Child. He was planning to dismiss Mary quietly rather than exposing her to the penalty for adultery, which was stoning to death. Before he could do so, an angel appeared to him in a dream and told him to take Mary as his wife, for her Child had been conceived by the Holy Spirit. The angel also told Joseph that this Child, Whom he was to name Jesus, would save God's people from their sins and fulfill an ancient prophecy. Joseph obeyed the angel and took Mary as his wife. Near the end of Mary's pregnancy, the couple traveled to Bethlehem in obedience to a Roman decree ordering all inhabitants of Judea to register in their ancestral towns. In Bethlehem, Mary gave birth to Jesus in a stable and laid Him in a manger, for there was no room for the little family at the local inn. Angels appeared to shepherds keeping watch in a nearby field and announced to them the birth of the Savior. The shepherds hurried to Bethlehem to see the

Rosary Meditations

Child. They rejoiced in His presence, praised God, and spread the word about this amazing event. Mary watched and listened closely and pondered all these things in her heart. Meanwhile, travelers were approaching, magi from the East. They arrived in Jerusalem, asking where they might find the newborn King of the Jews. They had seen His star and had come to pay Him homage. King Herod and the rest of Jerusalem were frightened by the magi's words. Herod called the chief priests and scribes and demanded to know where the Messiah was to be born. In Bethlehem of Judea, they told him. Herod called the magi to him and learned when the star had appeared. He ordered them to go and find the Child and then come back and tell him so that he might also pay Him homage. The magi found Jesus with his mother, Mary. They knelt before Him and presented their gifts of gold, frankincense, and myrrh. Then, warned by God in a dream not to return to Herod, they went back to their own country by another route.

Points to Ponder

1. Consider Joseph's predicament. Did he plan to dismiss Mary quietly because he believed her to be unfaithful, or did he perhaps feel unworthy to be the foster father of her Child?

2. Meditate on Joseph's dream, and think about the many ways in which God communicates with His people.

3. Joseph was obedient to the angel. He acted immediately and without question. He heard, and he responded. Ponder Joseph's readiness to obey God.

The Nativity

4. God often uses human events to accomplish His purposes. How did God work through the Roman emperor's decree?

5. Joseph and Mary went to Bethlehem to be registered because Joseph was a descendent of David. Jesus, too, was a descendent of David, legally through His foster father and probably by blood through His mother's line. Meditate on the importance of a Davidic Messiah.

6. The prophets foretold the coming of the Messiah. Read Isaiah 7:14, Isaiah 11:1-5, and Micah 5:2-5, and meditate on how Jesus fulfilled these prophecies.

7. There was no room for the Holy Family at the inn. Reflect deeply on this.

8. Jesus was born in poverty in a stable. Mary's joy was tinged with sorrow, for she was far from home and living in conditions far less than ideal. Why would the Messiah choose to come into the world in this way? How might the conditions of the stable mirror the conditions of a sinner's soul?

9. Jesus received some strange visitors during His first few hours and days of life. He was worshiped by the shepherds, the magi, and the angels. Meditate on the significance of each of these groups. Why were they chosen by God to be the first to encounter the Messiah?

10. When the angels announced the birth of the Savior to the shepherds, the latter experienced a wide range of reactions including fear, awe, and joy. God broke into the everyday lives of these humble people. They, in turn, immediately obeyed the angel's implicit command and

Rosary Meditations

set out to find the Child. Reflect on the shepherds and their actions.

11. The angel told the shepherds, "Do not be afraid." Ponder these simple yet significant words.

12. The angels understood the real meaning of Jesus' birth. They experienced awe in the true sense of the word. Meditate on this awe.

13. Read the Infancy Narratives (Luke 2:1-20 and Matthew 1:18-2:9), and identify the titles given to Jesus. What do these titles tell us about Jesus and His mission?

14. The angel announced to the shepherds that the Messiah would be a Savior for all people. How is this message good news of great joy for the whole world?

15. Meditate on each word of the angels' song in Luke 2:14. How do these few words manifest perfect praise?

16. Reflect on the significance of the manger. The One Who would become the Bread of Life slept in a manger used for feeding animals.

17. Think about God as a tiny, newborn Baby.

18. Mary pondered all these things in her heart. What things? What does it mean to ponder? How might Mary's pondering be a model for the Rosary prayer?

19. The shepherds, embracing faith and worshiping God, acted as missionaries and spread the message of the Messiah's birth. Consider how these lowly men had been changed by their encounter with the newborn King.

The Nativity

10. How do you follow Mary's example and treasure all the words of God, pondering them in your heart?

11. How do you praise God every day?

12. What gifts do you have to present to the Lord?

Prayer, Prayer, and More Prayer

Blessing and Adoration – We bless You, Lord, and we adore You, for You came among us as a Man, as our Emmanuel, as our Savior and King. Along with the shepherds and the magi, we bow down before You in silent adoration, offering You all that we have and all that we are. We love You, Lord.

Praise – We praise You, Jesus, and we sing to Your glory in imitation of the angels who announced Your birth that holy night. In Your greatness, You became small. In Your power, You became weak. And You did it all for us. You are truly awesome, God!

Thanksgiving – Lord, how can we ever thank You enough for the blessings You have poured out upon us through Your Incarnation and birth? We thank You anyway, even in our feebleness and with our stammering words. We thank You, too, for Your loving care and for the way You guide our lives.

Intercession – Lord, we lift up to You all those who are trying to find their way to You. Please guide them along the right path. We lift up those simple people who hear Your message and obey. May we learn from their example. We lift up all those who live in poverty. Please give them comfort in knowing that You were also poor

Rosary Meditations

and that You understand their situation. Please help them to trust You. We lift up those who refuse to acknowledge You and those who resort to deception to attain their own ends. May they come to know You and Your truth.

Petition – Jesus, may we always have room for You in our inns. May we always follow Your guidance in our lives. May we always give You our very best gifts. May we always ponder Your words and treasure them in our hearts.

Quotes from the Saints

"But if [Joseph] had no suspicion of her, how could he be a just man and yet seek to put her away, being immaculate? He sought to put her away, because he saw in her a great sacrament, to approach which he thought himself unworthy." – Origen

"It was the Lord who directed Augustus to give this edict, that he might minister to the coming of the Only-begotten; for it was this edict that brought Christ's mother into her country as the prophets had foretold, namely, to Bethlehem of Judea, according to the word, to a city of David, which is called Bethlehem." – St. John Chrysostom

"Bethlehem is by interpretation the house of bread. For it is the Lord Himself who says, *I am the bread of life which came down from Heaven*. The place therefore where the Lord was born was before called the house of bread, because it was there that He was to appear in His fleshly nature Who should refresh the souls of the elect with spiritual fullness." - St. Gregory the Great

The Nativity

"He is confined in the narrow space of a rude manger, Whose seat is the heavens, that He may give us ample room in the joys of His heavenly Kingdom. He Who is the bread of Angels is laid down in a manger, that He might feast us, as it were the sacred animals, with the bread of His flesh…He who sits at His Father's right hand, finds no room in an inn, that He might prepare for us in His Father's house many mansions; He is born not in His Father's house, but…by the way side, because through the mystery of the incarnation He was made the way by which to bring us to our country, (where we shall enjoy the truth and the life.)" - Theophylact

"It was in a mystery that the angel appeared to the shepherds while they were watching, and *the glory of the Lord shone round about them*, implying that they are thought worthy above the rest to see sublime things who take a watchful care of their faithful flocks; and while they themselves are piously watching over them, the Divine grace shines widely round about them." - St. Gregory the Great

"How remarkably Scripture weighs the import of each word. For when we behold the flesh of the Lord, we behold the Word, which is the Son. Let not this seem to you a slight example of faith, because of the humble character of the shepherds. For simplicity is sought for, not pride. It follows, *And they came in haste*. For no one indolently seeks after Christ." - St. Ambrose

Rosary Meditations

The Fourth Joyful Mystery: The Presentation of Jesus in the Temple

Scripture References

Luke 2:22-38; Leviticus 12:2-8

The Story in Brief

Jewish law required new mothers to be ritually purified by offering a sacrifice at the Temple in Jerusalem. Mary, always humble and obedient, went up to Jerusalem forty days after the birth of her Son to perform the ritual. Mary and Joseph also intended to present their firstborn Son to God, for all firstborn males were designated as holy to the Lord and had to be "redeemed" or "ransomed" through a ritual sacrifice. When the Holy Family arrived at the Temple, they found Simeon waiting for them. Simeon was a devout and righteous elderly man who was waiting and watching for the Messiah, for God had promised him that he would not die until he had seen the Savior. Led by the Holy Spirit, Simeon reached out for Jesus, took Him into his arms, praised God, and proclaimed a prophetic message concerning the infant Messiah. He also warned Mary that she would experience great sorrow as the mother of the Savior. A sword would pierce her soul. As Simeon finished speaking, an old woman named Anna

Rosary Meditations

approached the group. Anna always remained in the Temple, fasting and praying. Now she praised God and immediately began to spread the word to all who would listen that the Messiah had come.

Points to Ponder

1. Mary and Joseph obeyed the Law even though it did not technically apply to them. Mary was already pure, for Jesus was conceived by the power of the Holy Spirit. Jesus, the Son of God, was already completely and totally dedicated to the Father. Why, then, did the Holy Family go up to Jerusalem to perform the proper rituals?

2. Consider the irony of the immaculate Mary submitting to ritual purification.

3. Reflect on the amazing truth that Jesus, the Son of God, assumed our humanity and entered into our condition. Think about how Jesus identifies with us completely.

4. Mary and Joseph took Jesus to the Temple in order to present Him to the Lord. God was being presented to God. Ponder this.

5. The Holy Spirit rested on Simeon and guided him. Think about Simeon's intimate relationship with God.

6. Meditate on what it means to be righteous (i.e., right with God and conforming to God's will).[4]

7. Ponder what it means to be devout (i.e, correctly performing what is right in religion, behaving morally,

The Presentation

maintaining a healthy fear of the Lord, and fulfilling the duties of piety and humanity).[5]

8. Simeon trusted in God's promise that a Messiah would come to comfort and restore Israel. The word "consolation" implies an invitation or summons to God's side.[6] Ponder the depths of the "consolation of Israel."

9. Simeon had received a revelation that he would not die until he had seen the Messiah. He was ready; he was watching; he was waiting. He trusted, and he believed. Reflect on this special grace and on Simeon's response.

10. Consider Simeon's immediate obedience when the Holy Spirit prompted him to enter the Temple.

11. Simeon recognized the baby Jesus as the Messiah and approached the Holy Family. Imagine Simeon's reaction when he saw Jesus for the first time.

12. What did Simeon think and feel as he held God in his arms?

13. Simeon prophesied. He proclaimed truths that he could not have known except through the power of the Holy Spirit. Carefully consider Simeon's words in Luke 2:29-35.

14. Meditate on the titles Simeon used to describe Jesus (i.e, salvation, light, glory, etc.).

15. When Jesus came into the Temple, God arrived at His own house in an entirely new way. Ponder this amazing occurrence.

Rosary Meditations

16. Simeon proclaimed that God had prepared salvation for all people, including the Gentiles. Meditate on God's mercy to the world.

17. Why were Mary and Joseph amazed at Simeon's words? They already knew Who their Child was, but perhaps hearing anew the wonders of God's plan touched them in a powerful way.

18. Simeon blessed Mary and Joseph. A very holy man blessed two very holy people. Reflect on this blessing.

19. Simeon made a prediction to Mary. Jesus was destined for the rise and fall of many in Israel. He was a sign that would be opposed. Mary's heart would be pierced by a sword. Ponder how joy is often tinged with sorrow.

20. Simeon said that the inner thoughts of many would be revealed. The truth would be known. The heart would become prominent. Interior relationship with God would go hand in hand with exterior religious practice, and the external would spring from the internal. Reflect on these ideas.

21. Picture Anna. What was she like, this woman who had dedicated her entire life to God by remaining always in the Temple?

22. Notice Anna's worship, which incorporated both fasting and prayer. Think carefully about the relationship between fasting and prayer, between self-denial and self-offering, between letting go and letting God. How must one give up oneself to enter into a relationship with God?

The Presentation

23. Anna fasted and prayed night and day. Her focus was constantly on God. Reflect on Anna's dedication.

24. Anna became an evangelist. Ponder how she spoke about Jesus to others who were waiting for the redemption of Jerusalem.

25. How is Anna our role model? Think about her dedication, praise, evangelism, and enthusiasm.

Application Questions

1. How is the Holy Spirit working in your life? How is He guiding you? How are you responding?

2. How would you describe your relationship with God?

3. Are you righteous and devout in the sense described above? How might you become more so?

4. Are you watching and waiting for the Lord? Are you seeking Him with an open and willing heart?

5. Are you amazed by Jesus? What amazes you the most?

6. How often and in what ways do you bless those around you?

7. How has joy been tinged with sorrow in your life? What have you learned from those experiences?

8. Is your religious experience more internal or more external? Why? If you answered "external," how might you grow stronger in your interior relationship with God?

Rosary Meditations

9. Have you ever felt as though you have been pierced by a sword all the way to the depths of your soul? How did that experience affect your relationship with God?

10. How do you combine fasting and prayer? How might you fast and pray more frequently and more devoutly?

11. Have you dedicated your life to God? Why or why not? How might you either do so or deepen your dedication?

12. How do you spread the word about God and His plan for His people?

13. Do you get excited about God? Why or why not?

14. What lessons have you learned from Simeon and Anna?

<u>Prayer, Prayer, and More Prayer</u>

Blessing and Adoration – Lord, You came to Your Temple in a way no one expected. You came as a tiny, helpless baby. We adore You, little Jesus, and we bless You. We bow our heads in silent adoration as we contemplate You resting in Simeon's arms.

Praise – Jesus, You are amazing. You are the salvation of the world. You are the light for revelation to the Gentiles. You are the glory of Israel. You are the One destined for the rise and fall of many in Israel. You are the sign that would be opposed. You are the One Who causes the inner thoughts of many to be revealed. We praise You, Lord Jesus, for Who You are.

The Presentation

Thanksgiving – O Jesus, how can we ever thank You enough for all You have done for us? We thank You for coming among us as a human being, like us in all things except sin. We thank You for coming to save us. We thank You for keeping Your promises in such marvelous ways. We thank You for sending the Holy Spirit to guide us. We thank You for saints like Simeon and Anna who go before us in holiness to show us the way to You.

Intercession – Lord, we lift up to You all young families. Please infuse them with Your love. We lift up mothers who are experiencing sorrow in some way on account of their children. Comfort them, Lord. We lift up the elderly. Draw them close to You, Lord. We lift up those who have dedicated themselves completely to You as priests and religious men and women. Keep them strong in their vocations.

Petition – Jesus, please guide us through Your Holy Spirit, and open our hearts that we may follow His guidance. Help us to increase and strengthen our prayers and fasts and to improve our attention and devotion. Inspire us, Lord, to dedicate our entire lives to You and to spread Your word to those around us.

Quotes from the Saints

"But let us see what these offerings mean. The turtle dove is the most vocal of birds, and the pigeon the gentlest. And such was the Savior made unto us; He was endowed with perfect meekness, and like the turtle dove entranced the world, filling His garden with His own melodies. There was killed then either a turtle dove or a pigeon, that by a figure He might be shown forth to us as about to suffer in the flesh for the life of the world." - St. Cyril

Rosary Meditations

"Not only did Angels and Prophets, the shepherds and his parents, bear witness to the birth of the Lord, but the old men and the righteous. As it is said, *And, behold, there was a man in Jerusalem whose name was Simeon, and he was a just man, and one who feared God*. For scarcely is righteousness preserved without fear, I mean not that fear which dreads the loss of worldly goods, (which perfect love casts out) but that holy fear of the Lord which abides for ever, by which the righteous man, the more ardent his love to God, is so much the more careful not to offend Him." - St. Ambrose

"Hereby also we learn with what desire the holy men of Israel desired to see the mystery of His incarnation." - St. Gregory the Great

"To see death means to undergo it, and happy will he be to see the death of the flesh who has first been enabled to see with the eyes of his heart the Lord Christ, having his conversation in the heavenly Jerusalem, and frequently entering the doors of God's temple, that is, following the examples of the saints in whom God dwells as in His temple. By the same grace of the Spirit whereby he foreknew Christ would come, he now acknowledges Him come, as it follows, *And he came by the Spirit into the temple*." - Theophylact

"If we marvel to hear that a woman was healed by touching the hem of a garment, what must we think of Simeon, who received an Infant in his arms, and rejoiced seeing that the little One he carried was He Who had come to let loose the captive! Knowing that no one could release him from the chains of the body with the hope of future life, but He Whom he held in his arms. Therefore it

The Presentation

is said, *And he blessed God, saying, Lord, now let Your servant depart.*" - Origen

"Though these things are said of the Son, yet they have reference also to His mother, who takes each thing to herself, whether it be of danger or glory. He announces to her not only her prosperity, but her sorrows; for it follows, *And a sword shall pierce through your own heart.*" - St. Gregory of Nyssa

Rosary Meditations

The Fifth Joyful Mystery: The Finding of Jesus in the Temple

Scripture References

Luke 2:41-52

The Story in Brief

Every year, the Holy Family traveled to Jerusalem for the feast of Passover. When Jesus was twelve years old, He went with His parents as usual, but this time, Jesus stayed behind in Jerusalem when the rest of the company started for home. His parents, thinking He was with friends or relatives, did not realize He was missing until they had traveled for a day. Then they hurried back to look for their Son. After three days, they found Him in the Temple, conversing with the teachers. Everyone was amazed at Jesus' answers and understanding. His mother asked Him, "Child, why have You treated us like this? Look, Your father and I have been searching for You with great anxiety." Jesus answered, "Why were you searching for Me? Did you not know that I must be in My Father's house?" He returned to Nazareth with His parents and was obedient to them. Mary treasured her experiences with her Son and pondered them in her heart.

Rosary Meditations

Points to Ponder

1. Once again, the Holy Family faithfully followed the Jewish Law. They actually went beyond the letter of the Law when the whole family traveled to Jerusalem to observe the feast of Passover. Only adult males were required to go. What does this tell us about the Holy Family?

2. Reflect on the symbolism of Passover. Think about how this Jewish feast was transformed by Jesus, Who is the new Passover Lamb.

3. The Jerusalem Temple was the center of Jewish worship. Why was the Temple so important to the Jewish people, including the Holy Family?

4. This mystery stresses the necessity of proper worship. God has ordained specific ways for people to worship Him. These are not optional; they are intended for humankind's well-being and salvation. God required the Jewish people to observe certain feasts, offer sacrifices, and travel to Jerusalem at various times during the year. God requires Catholic Christians to assist at Mass on Sundays and Holy Days of Obligation. Ponder these truths.

5. In Jewish Law, boys reached adulthood at age twelve, so the twelve-year-old Jesus was legally a man able to take responsibility for His own deeds.[7] How did Jesus' age and status affect His words and actions during and after this Passover?

6. Why did Jesus stay behind in Jerusalem? Was He ready to begin His mission? Was He acting prophetically?

The Finding of Jesus in the Temple

Was He motivated by something else entirely or a combination of many things?

7. Any parent who loses a child, even for a little while, is terrified, but Mary and Joseph's anxiety was probably much greater than normal because they knew Who their Child was: the Messiah. Reflect on Mary and Joseph's fear.

8. Ponder what it means to lose Jesus and to seek Him.

9. Reflect on Mary and Joseph's search for Jesus. It was an orderly search. They checked with friends and relatives first. Then they went back to Jerusalem and finally to the Temple. How might this search be a metaphor for a person's journey to God?

10. Jesus was missing three days. Reflect on the significance of this.

11. Jesus carried on a dialogue with the teachers at the Temple. He listened to them, asked them questions, and answered their questions. Meditate on this dialogue. What was Jesus asking? Why does the Gospel not include the conversation word for word?

12. Think about how prayer and study ought to be a dialogue with God.

13. Everyone who heard Jesus was amazed at His answers and understanding. Imagine their reactions to the teaching of this twelve-year-old Boy.

14. Why were Mary and Joseph astonished by Jesus' teachings in Temple? They knew their Son well, and they

certainly remembered all that had happened at His birth. So why were they surprised?

15. Consider Mary's gentle rebuke. Remember, she was still a mother, and she must have been rather hurt by Jesus' actions.

16. Think about Jesus' response to Mary. How did it serve as a gentle reminder of Who He was and what He had come to do?

17. Jesus told Mary and Joseph that He had to be in His Father's house. In other translations, Jesus said that He had to be about His Father's business. What did Jesus mean? How do these two translations bring out different aspects of Jesus' words?

18. Why did Jesus' parents not understand Him?

19. Jesus left Jerusalem with Mary and Joseph, went back to Nazareth, and was obedient to them. God-made-Man submitted with great humility to His human parents. Ponder this.

20. Reflect on how Mary treasured all these things in her heart. She pondered deeply, knowing that God was active in her life and speaking to her through each and every event. She "mined" meaning from every occurrence and searched untiringly for God's message.

21. Ponder how Jesus grew, increasing in wisdom and age. Jesus was fully Man as well as fully God. He had a human soul and a human will as well as a human body. In His divine nature, He did not change, but in His human

The Finding of Jesus in the Temple

nature, He did. Think carefully about this great mystery of the God-Man.

Application Questions

1. How do you worship the Lord? Do you understand the importance of formal, ritualized worship? Do you attend Mass on Sundays and Holy Days? Are you typically focused or distracted at Mass? How might you pray better and be more attentive at Mass?

2. Have you ever experienced the fear of losing a child, even for a short time? How did you respond?

3. Have you ever lost Jesus? What did it feel like to lose Him?

4. How do you search for Jesus? What does it feel like to find Him?

5. How does Jesus carry on a dialogue with You? Are your prayer and study a dialogue with God?

6. How do you listen to God?

7. How does God question You? How do you respond?

8. What kinds of questions do you ask God? How does He answer?

9. Are you amazed by Jesus? What amazes you the most?

10. How are you going about your Father's business?

11. Do you always understand what Jesus tells you? What do you do when you do not understand?

12. Do you look for deeper meanings in the events of your life? Do you recognize God at work? Do you treasure even small things because God is directing them and speaking to you through them? Can you think of any events in your life that turned out to be much more meaningful than you realized at first?

Prayer, Prayer, and More Prayer

Blessing and Adoration – Dearest Jesus, we kneel before You in silent adoration, blessing You for Your wisdom and love. We pour out our hearts to You in worship, Jesus, our God, with the Father and the Holy Spirit.

Praise – Jesus, You are amazing! We are amazed by Your teaching, by Your wisdom, and by the answers You give us when we pray to You. Your words are simple yet sublime, and we praise You for each and every one of them. May they sink deeply into our hearts and minds, Lord Jesus.

Thanksgiving – Dearest Jesus, we thank You for all the opportunities You give us for prayer and study. We thank You for dialoguing with us. We thank You for giving us an example of humility and obedience. We thank You for showing us, Lord, that if we seek You, we will always find You, and when we do find You, we will be with You in Your Father's house and about Your Father's business.

Intercession – Lord, we lift up to You all children who are separated from their parents and loved ones. Please bring them home safely. We lift up to You all parents who are

The Finding of Jesus in the Temple

desperately seeking missing children. Please give them strength, courage, and perseverance, and comfort them in their time of anxiety and sorrow.

Petition – Jesus, help us to search for You and always to find You. Help us to pray and worship in the ways You ordain for us, in the ways that are pleasing to You. Help us to ponder all Your words and actions in our hearts, to treasure them and make them part of our very being. Help us to see the deep meanings in the events of our lives.

Quotes from the Saints

"Now that the Lord came up every year to Jerusalem at the Passover, betokens His humility as a man, for it is, man's duty to meet together to offer sacrifices to God, and conciliate Him with prayers. Accordingly the Lord as man, did among men what God by angels commended men to do. Hence it is said, *According to the custom of the feast day*. Let us follow then the journey of His mortal life, if we delight to behold the glory of His divine nature."
- Theophylact

"He is not found as soon as sought for, for Jesus was not among His kinsfolk and relations, among those who are joined to Him in the flesh, nor in the company of the multitude can He be found. Learn where those who seek Him find Him, not every where, but in the temple. And do you then seek Jesus in the temple of God. Seek Him in the Church, and seek Him among the masters who are in the temple. For if you wilt so seek Him, you shall find Him. They found Him not among His kinsfolk, for human relations could not comprehend the Son of God; not among His acquaintance, for He passes far beyond all human knowledge and understanding. Where then do they find Him? In the temple! If at any time you seek the Son of God, seek Him first in the temple, thither go up, and verily shall you find Christ, the Word, and the Wisdom (i.e., the Son of God.)" - Origen

"After three days He is found in the temple, that it might be for a sign, that after three days of victorious suffering, He Who was believed to be dead should rise again and manifest Himself to our faith, seated in heaven with divine glory." - St. Ambrose

"Because moreover He was the Son of God, He is found in the midst of the doctors, enlightening and instructing them. But because He was a little child, He is found among them not teaching but asking questions, as it is said, *Sitting in the midst of the doctors, hearing them, and asking them questions.* And this He did as a duty of reverence, that He might set us an example of the proper behavior of children, though they be wise and learned, rather to hear their masters than teach them, and not to vaunt themselves with empty boasting. But He asked not that He might learn, but that asking He might instruct." - Origen

"To show that He was a man, He humbly listened to the masters; but to prove that He was God, He divinely answered those who spoke." - Theophylact

"But from His very first years being obedient to His parents, He endured all bodily labors, humbly and reverently. For since His parents were honest and just, yet at the same time poor, and ill supplied with the necessaries of life, (as the stable which administered to the holy birth bears witness,) it is plain that they

The Finding of Jesus in the Temple

continually underwent bodily fatigue in providing for their daily wants. But Jesus being obedient to them, as the Scriptures testify, even in sustaining labors, submitted Himself to a complete subjection." - St. Basil

"The Virgin, whether she understood or whether she could not yet understand, equally laid up all things in her heart for reflection and diligent examination. Hence it follows, *And His mother laid up all these things*, etc. Mark the wisest of mothers, Mary the mother of true wisdom, becomes the scholar or disciple of the Child. For she yielded to Him not as to a boy, nor as to a man, but as unto God. Further, she pondered upon both His divine words and works, so that nothing that was said or done by Him was lost upon her, but as the Word itself was before in her womb, so now she conceived the ways and words of the same, and in a manner nursed them in her heart. And while indeed she thought upon one thing at the time, another she wanted to be more clearly revealed to her; and this was her constant rule and law through her whole life." - Theophylact

Rosary Meditations

The First Luminous Mystery: The Baptism of Jesus

Scripture References

Matthew 3:12-17; Mark 1:9-11; Luke 3:21-22; John 1:29-34

The Story in Brief

When John the Baptist was preaching and baptizing at the Jordan River, Jesus came from Galilee to be baptized. John was hesitant. He argued that Jesus ought to be baptizing him instead of the other way around, but Jesus assured John that His baptism was part of God's plan, so John consented. As Jesus was coming up out of the water, praying, the heavens opened above Him. The Holy Spirit descended in the form of a dove and landed on Jesus, and a voice boomed, "This is My Son, the Beloved, with Whom I am well pleased." Later, John testified to the event, declaring that Jesus, the Son of God, is also the Lamb of God Who will take away the sins of the world and baptize with the Holy Spirit.

Points to Ponder

1. Read the passages about John the Baptist in Matthew 3:1-12; Mark 1:1-8; and Luke 1:5-24, 1:39-45, 1:57-80, and 3:1-20. Who was John the Baptist as a person? What

Rosary Meditations

was he like? Why and how did he preach? What was his message? What role did he play in the divine plan of salvation history? How did people respond to him?

2. John was baptizing at the Jordan River, which is mentioned approximately 175 times in the Old Testament and 15 times in the New Testament.[8] The Jordan was the site of several miracles: the Israelites' crossing in Joshua 3:15-17; Naaman's healing in 2 Kings 5; and the floating axehead in 2 Kings 6:1-7. Why did John choose to baptize at the Jordan River?

3. John's baptism was one of repentance. It was a precursor to Christian baptism. Why was such a preparation necessary?

4. Why did Jesus come from Galilee to be baptized by John?

5. John humbly tried to decline Jesus' request for baptism. Why did he do that?

6. Jesus said, "Let it be so now; for it is proper for us in this way to fulfill all righteousness." Ponder this command.

7. The words "Let it be" or "suffer it to be" can denote "permitting" but also "letting go."[9] Reflect on how John had to let go of his own ideas and accept Jesus' way of doing things.

8. "Let it be so *now*..." God was doing something new at that moment in salvation history. Jesus focused John's attention on the present moment and His desire to share

The Baptism of Jesus

in the human condition. Meditate on Jesus' baptism as part of His participation in human nature.

9. "It is proper" indicates that a particular act is fitting for the moment. It is the right thing to do, and it suits the situation. Ponder Jesus' reassurance to John that His baptism was the right way to respond to God's will.

10. "In this way to fulfill all righteousness..." The Navarre Bible commentary notes, "'Righteousness (or 'justice') has a very deep meaning in the Bible; it refers to the plan which God, in His infinite goodness and wisdom, has marked out for man's salvation. Consequently, 'to fulfill all righteousness' should be understood as fulfilling God's will and designs. Thus we could translate 'fulfill all righteousness' as; 'fulfill everything laid down by God'. Jesus comes to receive John's baptism and hence recognizes it as a stage in salvation history – a stage foreseen by God as a final and immediate preparation for the messianic era....Jesus, Who has come to fulfill His Father's will, is careful to fulfill that saving plan in all its aspects."[10] Reflect carefully on these words.

11. John baptized Jesus. He accepted a mystery. He could not see the whole situation clearly, but he surrendered his own will and embraced God's will. Meditate on John's trust and obedience.

12. Reflect on Jesus' actual baptism. Picture yourself floating down into the peaceful waters with Jesus.

13. Baptism was a spiritual experience for Jesus, a deep, intimate point of communion with His Father. Ponder Jesus at prayer.

Rosary Meditations

14. The Holy Spirit descended and the Father spoke just as Jesus was coming up out of the water. Picture this scene.

15. The heavens were opened. Mark's word choice suggests that they were "torn apart." The same Greek word is used in Matthew 27:51, Mark 15:38, and Luke 23:45 to describe the tearing of the Temple curtain when Jesus died. Ponder the significance of this.

16. The Holy Spirit descended like a dove and landed on Jesus. Why did the Spirit choose the form of a dove? Meditate on the symbolism of the dove.

17. The voice from Heaven spoke: "This is My Son, the Beloved, with Whom I am well pleased" (in Matthew). Mark and Luke portray the Father as speaking directly to Jesus: "You are My Son, the Beloved; with You I am well pleased." Why is there a difference?

18. The Greek word for "beloved," *agapetos*, suggests a relationship between the Father and the Son that is pure love, deeper love than we can ever understand.[11] Ponder this extreme love.

19. What does the title "Beloved Son" tell us about Jesus?

20. The Father was well pleased with Jesus. The Greek verb for "to be well pleased," *eudokeo*, can also mean "to be delighted."[12] Because of Jesus, we, too, can be the beloved children of God with whom He is well pleased and even delighted. Meditate on this truth.

21. Ponder Jesus' baptism as an epiphany, a revelation of God, and a portrait of the Trinity.

The Baptism of Jesus

22. Meditate on how God broke into the world at the baptism of Jesus. Eternity broke into time, the divine into the mundane.

23. Do you think others heard the voice from Heaven or saw the dove? If so, how did they react? If not, why not?

24. John's Gospel does not describe Jesus' baptism, but it does recount John the Baptist's testimony about Jesus. When John saw Jesus coming toward him, he proclaimed to all who could hear that this One was the Lamb of God Who would take away the sins of the world. Ponder this sacrificial language that looks ahead toward the cross.

25. John said that he was baptizing so that Jesus might be revealed to Israel. How did John's baptism reveal Jesus to Israel?

26. Meditate on John's humility as he proclaimed that Jesus ranked ahead of him because He was before him.

27. Reflect on how John was always focused on Jesus and how he moved out of the way so that Jesus could take control.

28. John had received a prophecy from God. When he saw the Spirit descending from Heaven and remaining on Someone, he would know that this One would baptize with the Holy Spirit. Ponder this prophecy and its fulfillment. What does it mean to be baptized with the Holy Spirit?

29. Reflect on John's testimony that Jesus is the Son of God.

Rosary Meditations

30. In his testimony, John interpreted the events he had witnessed. He brought together history and mystery. Think deeply about John's interpretation of Jesus' baptism.

31. Benedict XVI offers an interpretation of Jesus' baptism that focuses on Jesus' solidarity with humanity. At the baptism, Benedict says, Jesus took upon Himself all our burdens and brought them down into the Jordan. He symbolically accepted "death for the sins of humanity" in a way that foreshadowed His death on the cross. Ponder Jesus' baptism as an identification and an anticipation.[13]

32. Many saints have pointed out that, through His baptism, Jesus prepared the way for the Christian sacrament of baptism. How did Jesus do this?

Application Questions

1. How would you have responded to John the Baptist and his preaching if you had lived in the first century?

2. How do you respond to John the Baptist and his preaching now? What message does he hold for your life today?

3. Have you ever experienced a time when you had to let go of your way of thinking and allow God to take over? What was that like? How did it change your relationship with God?

4. Do you believe that God has a plan for your life? Why or why not?

The Baptism of Jesus

5. How well do you accept mysteries?

6. How strong is your relationship with the Holy Spirit? How might that relationship grow and become stronger?

7. Do you understand that you are God's beloved child? How would this truth change your life if you kept it always in mind?

8. Are you following God's will in your life? How do you discern His will?

9. How does God reveal Himself to you? In what ways does He break into your world?

10. When, where, and how do you testify to Jesus?

11. Where can you see the mystery hidden in the history of the Scriptures?

12. What does your own baptism mean to you?

<u>Prayer, Prayer, and More Prayer</u>

Blessing and Adoration – Dearest Jesus, You are the Lamb of God Who takes away the sins of the world. You died that we might live with You and the Father and the Holy Spirit for all eternity. We bow our heads in silent adoration, Lord, as we contemplate Your baptism in the Jordan and the miraculous revelation of the Holy Trinity that accompanied the event.

Praise – Jesus, our Lord and our Savior, we praise You and we love You, for You have taken our sins upon Your shoulders. You identify with us in our burdens and trials,

Rosary Meditations

Lord, and You raise us up with You to the glory of Heaven. You are truly awesome, Jesus our God!

Thanksgiving – Lord God, we thank You for revealing Yourself to us in so many ways. Jesus, we thank You for submitting to baptism to fulfill all righteousness in the plan of salvation. Father, we thank You for speaking aloud at Jesus' baptism and declaring Him to be Your Beloved Son with Whom You are well pleased. Holy Spirit, we thank You for descending upon Jesus in the form of a dove and remaining on Him as a sign that He is the One Who baptizes us in Your power and love.

Intercession – Lord, we lift up to You all those who are preparing for baptism. We lift up parents who are getting ready to have their little ones baptized. We lift up those who are newly baptized. Please help them all to realize that baptism makes us beloved children of God.

Petition – Jesus, help us to fulfill Your will in all things, even when we cannot clearly see the path ahead of us or understand what You are doing. Help us to hear You and understand You when You reveal Yourself to us. Help us to truly believe that You are the One Who takes away our sins and baptizes us in the Holy Spirit. We love You, Jesus.

Quotes from the Saints

"Scripture tells of many wonders wrought at various times in this river; as that, among others, in the Psalms, Jordan was driven backwards (Psalms 114:3); before the water was driven back, now sins are turned back in its current; as Elijah divided the waters of old, so Christ the

The Baptism of Jesus

Lord wrought in the same Jordan the separation of sin." - St. Ambrose

"The Savior willed to be baptized not that He might Himself be cleansed, but to cleanse the water for us. From the time that Himself was dipped in the water, from that time has He washed away all our sins in water. And let none wonder that water, itself corporeal substance, is said to be effectual to the purification of the soul; it is so effectual, reaching to and searching out the hidden recesses of the conscience. Subtle and penetrating in its own nature, made yet more so by Christ's blessing, it touches the hidden springs of life, the secret places of the soul, by virtue of its all-pervading dew. The course of blessing is even yet more penetrating than the flow of waters. Thus the blessing which like a spiritual river flows on from the Savior's baptism, has filled the basins of all pools, and the courses of all fountains." - St. Augustine

"Beautifully said is that now, to show that as Christ was baptized with water by John, so John must be baptized by Christ with the Spirit. Or, suffer now that I who have taken the form of a servant should fulfill all that low estate; otherwise know that in the day of judgment you must be baptized with my baptism. Or, the Lord says, *'Suffer this now*; I have also another baptism wherewithal I must be baptized; you baptize Me with water, that I may baptize you for Me with my own blood.'" - St. Jerome

"Christ after He had been once born among men, is born a second time in the sacraments, that as we adore Him then born of a pure mother, so we may now receive Him immersed in pure water. His mother brought forth her Son, and is yet virgin; the wave washed Christ, and is holy. Lastly, that Holy Spirit which was present to Him in the womb, now shone round Him in the water, He Who then made Mary pure, now sanctifies the waters." - St. Augustine

"He witnesses that He is His Son not in name merely, but in very kindred. Sons of God are we many of us; but not as He is a Son, a proper and true Son, in verity, not in estimation, by birth, not adoption." - St. Hilary

"These words Mark and Luke give in the same way; in the words of the voice that came from Heaven, their expression varies though the sense is the same. For both the words as Matthew gives them, *This is My beloved Son*, and as the other two, *You are My beloved Son*, express the same sense in the speaker; (and the heavenly voice, no doubt, uttered one of these,) but one shows an intention of addressing the testimony thus born to the Son to those who stood by; the other of addressing it to Himself, as if speaking to Christ He had said, *This is My Son*. Not that Christ was taught what He knew before, but they who stood by heard it, for whose sake the voice came. Again, when one says, *in Whom I am well-pleased*; another, *in You it has pleased Me*, if you ask which of these was actually pronounced by that voice; take which you will, only remembering that those who have not related the same words as were spoken have related the same sense. That God is well-pleased with His Son is signified in the first; that the Father is by the Son pleased with men is conveyed in the second form, *in You it has well-pleased Me*. Or you may understand this to have been the one meaning of all the Evangelists, *In You have I put My good pleasure*, i.e., to fulfill all My purpose." - St. Augustine

The Second Luminous Mystery: The Wedding at Cana

Scripture References

John 2:1-12; Genesis 3:15; John 19:26

The Story in Brief

Early in His public ministry, Jesus, His mother, and His disciples were invited to a wedding at Cana in Galilee. When Jesus' mother discovered that the hosts had run out of wine, she came to Jesus and said, "They have no wine." At first, Jesus seemed to deny His mother's implicit request for help, but apparently their conversation extended beyond their words, for Mary instructed the servants, "Do whatever He tells you." Jesus told the servants to fill six stone jars with water. Then He commanded them to draw out some of the liquid and take it to the chief steward. The servants did so, and probably to their great relief, the chief steward discovered wine of superior quality. Jesus' glory was revealed, and His disciples began to believe in Him.

Points to Ponder

1. The wedding at Cana occurred on "the third day." Ponder the prophetic significance of this phrase. Why did

Rosary Meditations

John choose these words? How do they point toward the Resurrection?

2. In this story, John consistently refers to Mary as the "mother of Jesus" instead of calling her by her given name. Why?

3. Even though Mary was only a wedding guest, she discovered her hosts' dilemma. Meditate on Mary's loving attention to those around her.

4. Mary immediately approached Jesus on behalf of their hosts. Reflect on her prompt and loving intercession.

5. Running out of wine was an embarrassing problem for the hosts. Meditate on how Jesus and Mary care about all our problems and every aspect of our lives.

6. Mary's statement, "They have no wine," was simple. It was merely a statement, not even a request, but she knew her Son would respond. Ponder her deep and abiding trust in Jesus.

7. Jesus called his mother "woman." Read Genesis 3:15 and John 19:26, and ponder the connection of these passages with the current text. Scholars often use these three texts to show how Mary is our Coremptrix who merits, subordinately with Jesus, the graces of our redemption and then distributes those graces as our Mediatrix and prays for us as our Advocate.[14] Meditate on this Marian doctrine.

8. At first, Jesus seemed to respond unfavorably to Mary's implied request. Why did He do so? Why does

The Wedding at Cana

God, in His omniscience and mystery, sometimes delay answering prayers?

9. Jesus said, "Woman, what concern is that to you and to Me?" Why did He ask that?

10. Jesus continued, "My hour has not yet come." What did Jesus mean by this? One author suggests, "As of that moment, Jesus' hour had not yet come. But, once He performs the miracle, then His hour will begin. His march to the Cross will begin. A course will be set that will cause great suffering for both Him and His mother. I think Jesus simply wants to make sure that Mary truly understands what is about to happen and the full scope of her request."[15]

11. Think about the nonverbal conversation that took place between Jesus and Mary.

12. Mary said to the servants what she always says: "Do whatever He tells you." This is Mary's primary message, for she always directs our attention to her Son. Ponder this truth.

13. Consider Jesus' simple orders. He merely commanded the servants to fill the jars with water.

14. The servants immediately obeyed Jesus' orders even though they had no idea what He was going to do. They did not question Him. Reflect on their obedience.

15. The servants filled six stone water jars that were usually used for ritual purification. Why did Jesus put them to a new use? How was He suggesting the fulfillment and surpassing of Jewish rites?

Rosary Meditations

16. After the miracle, each stone jar held twenty to thirty gallons of wine, certainly more than necessary to satisfy the wedding party. Meditate on how God is extravagant in His answers to our prayers, how He lavishes good things upon us, and how He goes above and beyond our needs.

17. Jesus' second command was harder for the servants. There was some risk in drawing out liquid and taking it to the chief steward. The servants probably worried that they would look like fools for bringing their boss a drink of water, but they obeyed anyway without question. Why?

18. Think carefully about the miracle of water turned into wine. Jesus never touched the water. He did not speak any words over it. He silently willed it to be wine, and it was. Meditate on Jesus' power and complete control over the world around Him.

19. The water became wine of superior quality. What is the significance of this?

20. Think about the steward's cluelessness. He completely missed the miracle that had just occurred.

21. John makes a point of telling us that the servants knew where the wine had come from. Ponder how the lowly, the humble, and the obedient are blessed with faith and knowledge.

22. Recalling that Jesus is often referred to as "the Bridegroom," look deeply into this story about a wedding and a bridegroom to discover the message beneath its surface.

The Wedding at Cana

23. Ponder the symbolism of the water turned into wine. What might this miracle symbolize in the Church, in the Bible, in salvation history, and in our own lives?

24. Changing water into wine was the first of Jesus' signs (John's word for miracles). Why did Jesus choose this as His first sign? Ponder the purpose of signs, which point to something beyond themselves.

25. Jesus revealed His glory, and the disciples believed in Him. How was Jesus' glory revealed? What did the disciples believe?

26. Reflect on this mystery's message about marriage. Why is it significant that Jesus' first sign was performed in the context of a wedding celebration?

Application Questions

1. Do you immediately go to Jesus with any need or problem, even the small things? Why or why not?

2. How would you describe your relationship with Mary, the mother of God? Do you believe and understand that she loves you and intercedes for you?

3. Do you trust Jesus to respond to all your needs, explicit and implicit, spoken and unspoken? Why or why not? How does your trust, or lack thereof, affect your life? How might you grow in trust?

4. Has God ever seemed to delay answering your prayers or to not answer them at all? How did you feel? Why do you suppose God responded in the way He did? What

Rosary Meditations

lessons have you learned from seemingly unanswered prayers?

5. Do you ever share in nonverbal conversation with Jesus? Is your prayer ever beyond words? What is that experience like?

6. How do you imitate Mary in pointing to Jesus? How do you follow her command to "Do whatever He tells you"?

7. How has God been extravagant to you?

8. Have you ever noticed that God's commands are very simple yet are not always easy to fulfill? How can this be? Which of His commands are especially challenging to you?

9. Do you unquestioningly obey God even when you do not understand what He is doing or why He is doing it?

10. Do you believe that God is in control? How might your life and attitude be different if you kept this truth always in mind?

11. Are you humble enough to see miracles? Why or why not?

12. In which areas of your life do you need to ask Jesus to change water into wine?

Prayer, Prayer, and More Prayer

Blessing and Adoration – Lord Jesus, You turned water into wine by silently willing it. Your power and control

The Wedding at Cana

are greater than we can ever grasp. We bow our heads in silent adoration and worship You, our omnipotent God.

Praise – Jesus, we praise You for always answering our prayers, even when You give us an answer we do not expect. We praise You for changing water into wine, both at the wedding and in our lives. We praise You for Your power and Your glory and Your awesome signs, Lord Jesus.

Thanksgiving – Jesus, how can we ever thank You enough for Your answers to our prayers? We thank You for answering our largest prayers and our smallest ones. We thank You for answering our prayers even when You do so in ways we do not understand. We thank You for answering our prayers even when You say "no." Finally, we thank You for giving us Your mother, Mary, as our mother and intercessor.

Intercession – Lord, we lift up to You all newlyweds and those preparing for marriage. We lift up those who are lacking something they need, whether it is something major or minor. We lift up those who need to have the water of their lives changed into the wine of God's grace.

Petition – Jesus, help us to be obedient to You even when we do not understand Your commands. Inspire our hearts to recognize the needs of those around us and to intercede with You for them. Grant us, Lord, the kind of intimate communication with You that does not always require words but is a communion of hearts.

Rosary Meditations

Quotes from the Saints

"Nor is it without some mysterious allusion, that the marriage is related as taking place on the third day. The first age of the world, before the giving of the Law, was enlightened by the example of the Patriarchs; the second, under the Law, by the writings of the Prophets; the third, under grace, by the preaching of the Evangelists, as if by the light of the third day; for our Lord had now appeared in the flesh. The name of the place too where the marriage was held, Cana of Galilee, which means, desire of migrating, has a typical signification, viz. that those are most worthy of Christ, who burn with devotional desires, and have known the passage from vice to virtue, from earthly to eternal things." - St. Bede

"But how came it into the mother's mind to expect so great a thing from her Son? For He had done no miracle as yet: as we read afterwards *This beginning of miracles did Jesus*. His real nature, however, was beginning now to be revealed by John, and His own conversations with His disciples; besides that His conception, and the circumstances of His birth, had from the first given rise to high expectations in her mind: as Luke tells us, *His mother kept all these sayings in her heart*. Why then did she never ask Him to work a miracle before? Because the time had now come that He should be made known. Before He had lived so much like an ordinary person, that she had not had the confidence to ask Him. But now that she heard that John had borne witness to Him, and that He had disciples, she asks Him confidently." - St. John Chrysostom

"Water is poured into the waterpots; wine is drawn out into the chalices; the senses of the drawer out agree not

The Wedding at Cana

with the knowledge of the pourer in. The pourer in thinks that water is drawn out; the drawer out thinks that wine was poured in. When the ruler of the feast had tasted the water that was made wine, and knew not whence it was, (but the servants who drew the water knew,) the governor of the feast called the bridegroom. It was not a mixture, but a creation: the simple nature of water vanished, and the flavor of wine was produced; not that a weak dilution was obtained, by means of some strong infusion, but that which was, was annihilated; and that which was not, came to be." - St. Hilary

"Our Lord wished the power of His miracles to be seen gradually; and therefore He did not reveal what He had done Himself, nor did the ruler of the feast call upon the servants to do so; (for no credit would have been given to such testimony concerning a mere man, as our Lord was supposed to be) but he called the bridegroom, who was best able to see what was done. Christ moreover did not only make wine, but the best wine. And (the ruler of the feast) said to him, *Every man at the beginning does set forth good wine, and when men have well drunk, then that which is worse; but you have kept the good wine until now.* The effects of the miracles of Christ are more beautiful and better than the productions of nature. So then that the water was made wine, the servants could testify; that it was made good wine, the ruler of the feast and the bridegroom." - St. John Chrysostom

"But see the mysteries which lie hid in that miracle of our Lord. It was necessary that all things should be fulfilled in Christ which were written of Him: those Scriptures were the water. He made the water wine when He opened to them the meaning of these things, and expounded the Scriptures; for thus that came to have a taste which before had none, and that inebriated, which did not inebriate before." - St. Augustine

The Third Luminous Mystery: The Proclamation of the Kingdom and the Call to Conversion

Scripture References

Matthew 4:12-22; Matthew 5:1-7:29; Matthew 9:9-13; Matthew 13:1-50; Matthew 16:24-28; Matthew 18:1-5; Matthew 18:10-14; Matthew 18:23-35; Matthew 19:13-15; Matthew 20:1-16; Matthew 22:1-14; Mark 1:14-20; Mark 2:13-17; Mark 4:1-32; Mark 8:34-9:1; Mark 10:13-16; Luke 4:16-21; Luke 5:1-11; Luke 5:27-32; Luke 6:20-49; Luke 7:36-50; Luke 8:4-15; Luke 9:23-27; Luke 10:25-37; Luke 12:22-34; Luke 15:1-31; Luke 18:15-17; Luke 19:1-10; John 1:35-51; John 4:1-42; Acts 2:14-42; Acts 9:1-19

The Story in Brief

Unlike most other Rosary mysteries, the Proclamation of the Kingdom and the Call to Conversion does not refer to a single event in the lives of Jesus and Mary. Instead, it was, and is, an ongoing process that began early in Jesus' public ministry when He announced that the Kingdom of God was at hand. The process continued when Jesus called His disciples; when people like Zacchaeus, the Samaritan woman, and the sinful woman who wept at Jesus' feet turned their hearts to God; when Peter

Rosary Meditations

preached courageously after the Resurrection; and when Paul experienced his miraculous conversion. Even today, we are all called to set out on our own conversion journeys and to embrace the Kingdom of God.

Points to Ponder

1. This mystery invites us to pray the Bible. Open to one of the Scripture references listed above, read it slowly and carefully, and meditate on its message about the Kingdom of God and the call to conversion.

2. Reflect on Jesus' announcement that the Kingdom of God is at hand (see Matthew 4:12-17; Mark 1:14-15; and Luke 4:16-30). You might focus on some of the following ideas:
- Jesus as a great light
- Repentance
- The nearness of the Kingdom
- Jesus Himself as the Kingdom of God
- The fullness of time
- The fulfillment of Isaiah's prophecy as described in Luke
- The characteristics of the Kingdom as presented in Luke
- The persecution of Jesus as narrated in Luke
- The coming of the Kingdom to the Gentiles
- Jesus passing through the midst of the crowd and going away

3. Ponder the call of the first disciples (see Matthew 4:18-22; Mark 1:16-20; Luke 5:1-11; and John 1:35-51). Consider some of the following:
- Jesus' call to the disciples to fish for people

The Proclamation of the Kingdom

- The disciples' willingness to immediately leave their nets and their families to follow Jesus
- The strength of God's call
- The disciples' total surrender
- The miraculous catch in Luke
- Peter's obedience, astonishment, and fear in response to the miraculous catch
- God's lavishness
- Jesus' control and power
- The disciples' desire to stay with Jesus as described in John
- The disciples' realization that they had found the Messiah
- Simon's new name, "Peter"
- Nathanael's doubt and confession
- Jesus' prediction that the disciples would see Heaven opened and the angels of God ascending and descending upon the Son of Man

4. Think about the conversion of Matthew (see Matthew 9:9-13; Mark 2:13-17; and Luke 5:27-32). Reflect on how Jesus converted Matthew with only two simple words: "Follow Me." You might also consider the following:
- The nonverbal communication between Jesus and Matthew
- Matthew's outcast status as a tax collector
- Matthew's total surrender to Jesus
- Matthew's complete renunciation of his current life to become a disciple
- Matthew's missionary efforts
- Jesus' role as a physician
- Jesus' desire for mercy, not sacrifice

Rosary Meditations

- Jesus' violation of Jewish traditions when He ate with the "unclean"
- The Pharisees' question to the disciples
- The call to repentance

5. Read and ponder the Sermon on the Mount (see Matthew 5-7) and the Sermon on the Plain (see Luke 6:20-49). How do these sermons proclaim the Kingdom and call for conversion? Meditate on the following:
   - The beatitudes (Matthew) and the blessings and woes (Luke)
   - The metaphors of salt and light
   - Anger
   - Love for enemies
   - The Lord's Prayer
   - Almsgiving, fasting, and praying in secret
   - The inner room of the heart
   - Real treasure
   - Trust in God
   - God's mercy and human mercy
   - Jesus' prohibition against judging
   - Asking, seeking, and knocking
   - The golden rule
   - The narrow gate
   - Knowing a tree by its fruits
   - The house on the rock and the house on the sand

6. Reflect on Jesus' parables, which contain lessons about the Kingdom and stories of conversion. Choose one or more of the following:
   - The parable of the sower
   - The parable of the weeds among the wheat
   - The parable of the hidden treasure

The Proclamation of the Kingdom

- The parable of the net in the sea
- The parable of the fine pearl
- The parable of the lost sheep
- The parable of the unforgiving servant
- The parable of the laborers in the vineyard
- The parable of the wedding banquet
- The parable of the mustard seed
- The parable of the good Samaritan
- The parable of the lost coin
- The parable of the prodigal son

7. Think carefully about Jesus' blessing of the little children (see Matthew 19:13-15; Mark 10:13-16; and Luke 18:15-17). What does it mean to be like a little child? Meditate on the trust and innocence of little children.

8. Ponder Jesus' command to deny yourself, take up your cross, and follow Him (see Matthew 16:24-28 and Luke 9:23-27). This is the work of conversion. Reflect on how you actually find true life when you lose your life for Jesus' sake.

9. Consider the conversion story of the sinful woman in Luke 7:36-50. Think about some of the following:
   - The woman's internal repentance and her external manifestation of that repentance
   - Jesus' teaching about the relationship between forgiveness and love
   - The difference between the woman and Simon the Pharisee
   - The parable of the two forgiven debtors
   - Jesus' divine prerogative to forgive sins

Rosary Meditations

10. Ponder the conversion story of Zacchaeus in Luke 19:1-10. Be mindful of the following points: Zacchaeus was the chief tax collector, very rich, and, therefore, probably a crook; tax collectors were the lowest of the low among the Jews; and Zacchaeus was so drawn to Jesus that he risked looking like a fool and climbed a tree just to catch a glimpse of Him. Think also about how Jesus invited Himself to stay at Zacchaeus' house and about Zacchaeus' response of repentance and reparation for his sins. Consider how Jesus' mission was fulfilled in Zacchaeus.

11. Reflect on the story of the Samaritan woman in John 4:1-42. Meditate on some of the following:
    - The woman's gradual conversion
    - Jesus' frank but non-accusatory attitude about the woman's sins
    - Living water
    - Worship in spirit and truth
    - Jesus' revelation of Himself as the Messiah
    - The woman's role as an evangelist who drew others to Jesus
    - The conversion and testimony of the Samaritans

12. Consider Peter's message about the Kingdom in Acts 2:14-42. Reflect on the fulfillment of prophecies; the proclamation of Jesus as the Messiah; the conversion of three thousand; and the life of the first Christian community.

13. Ponder Paul's conversion in Acts 9:1-19. Think about some of the following:
    - Paul's physical blindness and former spiritual blindness

- Jesus' identification with the Church (i.e., to persecute the Church was to persecute Jesus)
- Fasting and prayer as part of conversion
- Ananias' vision
- Ananias laying hands on Paul
- People assisting one another along the path of conversion
- Jesus' desire to use Paul as His instrument
- Paul being filled with the Spirit
- The significance of something like scales falling from Paul's eyes
- The Eucharistic overtones of Paul taking food to regain his strength

Application Questions

1. What is your conversion story?

2. How are you growing closer to God each and every day?

3. In which areas of your life do you still need to convert, to turn away from sin and turn to God?

4. How do you experience the Kingdom of God?

5. How has God called you in the past? How is He calling you now? How do you respond?

6. Is there anything in your life that you need to leave behind in order to follow Jesus? What and why?

7. In which areas of your life do you need Jesus' healing touch?

Rosary Meditations

8. How might you apply the teachings of the Sermon on the Mount and the Sermon on the Plain to your own life?

9. How might you apply the lessons of the parables to your own life?

10. Are you ever like a little child? How so? How might you become more like a little child?

11. Do you take up your cross and follow Jesus each day? In what ways? What is your attitude toward the cross and toward trials in your life?

12. Do you need to repent of any sins? What are they?

13. Do you trust that Jesus will forgive your sins when you repent? How often do you go to confession? What is your attitude toward this sacrament?

14. How do you respond to Jesus' love and mercy?

15. Are you willing to look like a fool to follow Jesus?

16. How do you draw others to Jesus?

17. Are you ever spiritually blind? In what ways? Have you asked Jesus to open your eyes? Why or why not?

18. How do you pray and fast?

19. How do other people help you in your conversion? How do you help others?

The Proclamation of the Kingdom

<u>Prayer, Prayer, and More Prayer</u>

Blessing and Adoration – God, we bow our heads in silent adoration as we contemplate the Kingdom You have established and Your call to us to enter into relationship with You. We bless You, dearest Lord, and we worship You.

Praise – Jesus, Your teaching is amazing! You speak to us in ways that we can understand, through parables, through beatitudes, and through Your actions. We praise You for bringing the Kingdom to us and inviting us to enter into it to be with You forever.

Thanksgiving – Thank You, dearest Jesus, for inviting us to a life of conversion and for allowing us to experience Your Kingdom. Thank You for healing us, for teaching us, for showing us the way to You, and for gently guiding us along that way. We love You, Jesus.

Intercession – Jesus, we lift up to You all people who are following the path of conversion and seeking Your Kingdom. We lift up those who are currently leading a sinful life and pray that they may hear Your call in their hearts and turn away from their sins to follow You.

Petition – Lord, please guide all of us in our daily journey of conversion. Please bring us safely into Your Kingdom that we may live with You now and always. Please help us to not only hear Your teachings but to really understand them and follow them. Please give us the grace to repent of our sins and turn to You for forgiveness and eternal life.

Rosary Meditations

Quotes from the Saints

"Repent, therefore, and believe; that is, renounce dead works; for of what use is believing without good works? The merit of good works does not, however, bring to faith, but faith begins, that good works may follow." - St. Bede

"He chose not kings, senators, philosophers, or orators, but He chose common, poor, and untaught fishermen. Had one learned been chose, he might have attributed the choice to the merit of his learning. But our Lord Jesus Christ, willing to bow the necks of the proud, sought not to gain fishermen by orators, but gained an Emperor by a fisherman. Great was Cyprian the pleader, but Peter the fisherman was before him." - St. Augustine

"Peter and Andrew had seen Christ work no miracle, had heard from Him no word of the promise of eternal reward, yet at this single bidding of the Lord they forgot all that they had seemed to possess, and straightway left their nets, and followed Him. In which deed we ought rather to consider their wills than the amount of their property. He leaves much who keeps nothing for himself, he parts with much, who with his possessions renounces his lusts. Those who followed Christ gave up enough to be coveted by those who did not follow. Our outward goods, however small, are enough for the Lord; He does not weigh the sacrifice by how much is offered but out of how much it is offered. The Kingdom of God is not to be valued at a certain price, but whatever a man has, much or little, is equally available." - St. Gregory the Great

"Why is it then that nothing is said of the rest of the Apostles how or when they were called, but only of Peter,

The Proclamation of the Kingdom

Andrew, James, John, and Matthew? Because these were in the most alien and lowly stations, for nothing can He more disreputable than the office of Publican, nothing more abject than that of fisherman." - St. John Chrysostom

"Now our Lord while He ever raises us to look to the future reward of virtue, and teaches us how good it is to despise worldly things, so also He supports the weakness of the human mind by a present recompense. For it is a hard thing to take up the cross, and expose your life to danger and your body to death; to give up what you are, when you wish to be what you are not; and even the loftiest virtue seldom exchanges things present for future. The good Master then, lest any man should be broken down by despair or weariness, straightway promises that He will be seen by the faithful, in these words, *But I say to you, There are some standing here who shall not taste of death till they see the Kingdom of God.*" - St. Ambrose

"There are in truth three states of the converted: the beginning, the middle, and the perfection. In the beginning they experience the charms of sweetness; in the middle the contests of temptation; and in the end the fullness of perfection." - St. Gregory the Great

For more quotes from the saints, consult the *Catena Aurea* for each Scripture text listed.[16]

Rosary Meditations

The Fourth Luminous Mystery: The Transfiguration

Scripture References

Matthew 17:1-9; Mark 9:2-8; Luke 9:28-36

The Story in Brief

A few days after Jesus foretold His death and Resurrection and commanded His disciples to deny themselves, take up their crosses, and follow Him, He led Peter, James, and John up a high mountain to pray. The three disciples were sleepy but still awake when, suddenly, Jesus was transfigured before them. His face shone brightly, and His clothes became dazzlingly white. Moses and Elijah appeared next to Jesus and talked with Him about what was soon to happen in Jerusalem. Peter, overcome with awe, asked Jesus if he could make three tents, one for Him, one for Moses, and one for Elijah. He hardly knew what he was saying. While he was still speaking, a bright cloud overshadowed the group, and a voice rang out, "This is My Son, the Beloved, with Him I am well pleased; listen to Him!" The disciples were so frightened that they dropped to the ground. Jesus came over and touched His terrified disciples, telling them, "Get up and do not be afraid." When the disciples arose, they saw no one but Jesus. As they were coming down the mountain, Jesus ordered His disciples not to tell

Rosary Meditations

anyone about their experience until after He had been raised from the dead.

Points to Ponder

1. Consider the timing of the Transfiguration. Matthew and Mark tell us that it took place six days after Jesus foretold His death and Resurrection and commanded His disciples to deny themselves, take up their crosses, and follow Him. Luke indicates that eight days had passed. Why do you think the accounts differ? Some Fathers and scholars point to the Evangelists' different ways of reckoning time. Luke includes "bookend" days while Matthew and Mark do not.[17] Others focus on the symbolism of the numbers. The number six can symbolize the fullness of creation, for God created the world in six days. The number eight can symbolize the Resurrection, which occurred on the eighth day (or the day after the Sabbath) and points to a new creation.[18] In any case, reflect on God's perfect timing.

2. Think about Peter, James, and John, Jesus' inner circle among the apostles. Why did Jesus take only these three up the mountain? Carefully consider the wording here. Jesus took them *with Him*. Jesus was in the lead. The three apostles were following. Further, the Greek word for "to take," *paralambanō*, has connotations of drawing a person near to one's self (i.e, into a relationship).[19]

3. Matthew and Mark both emphasize that Peter, James, and John were with Jesus. Mark also includes the word "apart." Why do the evangelists specifically point out this separation from other people?

The Transfiguration

4. Luke adds that the group went up the mountain "to pray." How does this detail enhance the story of the Transfiguration, and why does Luke include it?

5. How was the Transfiguration a "mountain top" spiritual experience for both the disciples and Jesus?

6. Matthew and Mark use the word "transfigured" (the Greek verb *metamorphoō*) to describe Jesus' dazzling appearance, but Luke uses "altered" or "changed" (the Greek adjective *heteros*). Why did the evangelists choose different words? Keep in mind that Luke may be focusing on the "otherness" of Jesus during the Transfiguration, for his word strongly connotes a distinction.[20] Matthew and Mark's word appears only four times in the Gospels, twice to describe Jesus and twice to describe transformations in His disciples. What is significant about this?

7. Meditate on the changes in Jesus. His face shone like the sun, according to Matthew. Luke tells us that the appearance of His face was different and that Jesus' clothes became dazzling, glistening white. Mark adds that His garments became whiter than anyone on earth could bleach them. The light seemed to be coming from Jesus' very depths. He was radiating divinity, purity, and glory.

8. Think about Moses and Elijah. Many scholars say that they represent the Law and the prophets. Luke notes that they appeared in glory and were speaking about the "departure" that Jesus would accomplish in Jerusalem. Imagine their conversation with Jesus.

Rosary Meditations

9. Peter wanted to make three tents, one for Jesus, one for Moses, and one for Elijah. Some authors have suggested that with these words, Peter was recognizing Jesus as the Messiah Who would fulfill the expectations of the Feast of Tabernacles. During this feast, the Israelites constructed tents in remembrance of their time in the desert and in anticipation of the coming of the Messiah.[21] Reflect on Peter's request.

10. Luke adds that Peter did not really know what he was saying because the disciples were very sleepy (yet still awake). Think about how this detail points to an experience that was not a dream yet was far from ordinary.

11. Ponder the bright cloud that overshadowed the mountain. This was the *Shekinah* or glory cloud that signified God's presence. In Luke's account, the group on the mountain actually entered the cloud. This was something new. In the Old Testament, no one but Moses went into the *Shekinah*. Anyone else who tried would have died instantly, overcome by the power of God. Peter, James, and John, however, were with Jesus, so they could and did enter into the very presence of God.

12. Reflect on the words of God the Father: "This is My Son, the Beloved; with Him I am well pleased; listen to Him!" (see Matthew 17:5). What do these words tell us about the Father, the Son, and their relationship? Ponder what it means to listen to Jesus.

13. Consider the disciples' response to the Father's voice. They fell to the ground in terror.

The Transfiguration

14. Jesus touched His companions and told them to get up and not to be afraid. Consider the importance of touch, and meditate on how Jesus is fully God but also fully human.

15. Jesus told the disciples not to say anything about their experience until after the Resurrection. Why?

16. Why did Jesus allow the disciples to see Him transfigured?

Application Questions

1. How is God's timing at work in your life?

2. Do you realize that when you are in a state of grace, you are part of Jesus' inner circle? How does that intimate relationship affect every aspect of your life?

3. How much time do you spend alone with Jesus?

4. Have you had any "mountain top" spiritual experiences? What were they like?

5. How has Jesus transfigured you? How do you still need to change and be changed?

6. How have you experienced God's presence? Have you ever been overcome by God's awesomeness?

7. In what ways do you listen to Jesus? How might you learn to listen more and better?

8. How have you experienced Jesus' calming touch?

Rosary Meditations

<u>Prayer, Prayer, and More Prayer</u>

Blessing and Adoration – Dearest Jesus, on the mountain of the Transfiguration, Your face shone like the sun and Your garments became dazzling white. Your divinity shone through Your humanity. We bow our heads in silent adoration, Lord, as we contemplate the mystery of You, true God and true Man.

Praise – Jesus, You are the Father's beloved Son and our beloved Savior and Brother, and You are amazing! We praise You for Your glorious revelation to Peter, James, and John, and to us, in the Transfiguration. We praise You for assuming our human nature in order to save us from our sins and bring us home to Heaven to be with You and the Father and the Holy Spirit forever and ever.

Thanksgiving – Thank You, Jesus, for allowing us to catch little glimpses of Your awesomeness. Thank You for the "mountain top" experiences that we sometimes enjoy during our spiritual journey. Thank You, too, for the times when all seems dark and low because we know that You are with us even then and that You are holding us up and teaching us to follow You in love.

Intercession – Lord, we lift up to You all people who do not acknowledge You and Your constant, sustaining presence. Please give them faith and open their hearts so that they may come to believe in You and know that You are truly the Savior of the world. We lift up, too, those who are frightened of You for any reason. Please let them recognize Your gentle, loving care.

Petition – Transfigure us, Lord Jesus. Change us from the inside out. Cleanse us from our faults. Raise us from our

The Transfiguration

falls. Scour our souls that they may be white and bright and shining. Help us to always listen to You, as the Father commanded when He spoke out of the cloud, and draw us constantly into Your loving presence.

Quotes from the Saints

"Such as He is to be in the time of the Judgment, such was He now seen of the Apostles. Let none suppose that He lost His former form and lineaments, or laid aside His bodily reality, taking upon Him a spiritual or ethereal Body. How His transfiguration was accomplished, the Evangelist shows, saying, *And His face did shine as the sun, and His raiment became white as snow*. For that His face is said to shine, and His raiment described to become white, does not take away substance, but confer glory. In truth, the Lord was transformed into that glory in which He shall hereafter come in His Kingdom. The transformation enhanced the brightness, but did not destroy the countenance, although the body were spiritual; whence also His raiment was changed and became white to such a degree, as in the expression of another Evangelist, *no fuller on earth can whiten them*. But all this is the property of matter, and is the subject of the touch, not of spirit and ethereal, an illusion upon the sight only beheld in phantasm." - St. Jerome

"There are many reasons why these should appear. The first is this; because the multitudes said He was Elias, or Jeremiah, or one of the Prophets, He here brings with Him the chief of the Prophets, that hence at least may be seen the difference between the servants and their Lord. Another reason is this, because the Jews were ever charging Jesus with being a transgressor of the Law and blasphemer, and usurping to Himself the glory of the

Rosary Meditations

Father, that He might prove Himself guiltless of both charges, He brings forward those who were eminent in both particulars; Moses, who gave the Law, and Elias, who was jealous for the glory of God. Another reason is, that they might learn that He has the power of life and death; by producing Moses, who was dead, and Elias, who had not yet experienced death. A further reason also the Evangelist discovers, that He might show the glory of His cross, and thus soothe Peter, and the other disciples, who were fearing His death; for they talked, as another Evangelist declares, of His decease which He should accomplish at Jerusalem. Wherefore He brings forward those who had exposed themselves to death for God's pleasure, and for the people that believed; for both had willingly stood before tyrants, Moses before Pharaoh, Elias before Ahab. Lastly, also, He brings them forward, that the disciples should emulate their privileges, and be meek as Moses, and zealous as Elias." - St. John Chrysostom

"If the transfigured humanity of Christ and the society of but two saints seen for a moment, could confer delight to such a degree that Peter would, even by serving them, stay their departure, how great a happiness will it be to enjoy the vision of Deity amidst choirs of Angels for ever? It goes on, *For he wist not what to say*; although, however, Peter from the stupor of human frailty knew not what to say, still he gives a proof of the feelings which were within him; for the cause of his not knowing what to say, was his forgetting that the Kingdom was promised to the Saints by the Lord not in any earthly region, but in Heaven; he did not remember that he and his fellow-Apostles were still hemmed in by mortal flesh and could not bear the state of immortal life, to which his soul had already carried him away, because in our Father's house

The Transfiguration

in Heaven, a house made with hands is not needed. But again even up to this time he is pointed at, as an ignorant man who wishes to make three tabernacles for the Law, the Prophets, and the Gospel, since they in no way can be separated from each other." - St. Bede

"This is the Son, this the Beloved, this the Accepted; and He it is Who is to be heard, as the voice out of the cloud signifies, saying, *Hear you Him.* For He is a fit teacher of doing the things He has done, who has given the weight of His own example to the loss of the world, the joy of the cross, the death of the body, and after that the glory of the heavenly Kingdom." - St. Hilary

"Now observe, that the cloud was not black from the darkness of condensed air, and such as to overcast the sky with a horrible gloom, but a shining cloud, from which we were not moistened with rain, but as the voice of Almighty God came forth the dew of faith was shed upon the hearts of men. For it follows, *And there came a voice out of the cloud, saying, This is My beloved Son: hear you Him.* Elias was not His Son. Moses was not. But this is the Son Whom you see alone." - St. Ambrose

"And we must observe, that, as when the Lord was baptized in Jordan, so on the mountain, covered with brightness, the whole mystery of the Holy Trinity is declared, because we shall see in the Resurrection that glory of the Trinity which we believers confess in baptism, and shall praise it all together. Nor is it without reason that the Holy Ghost appeared here in a bright cloud, there in the form of a dove; because he who now with a simple heart keeps the faith which he has embraced, shall then contemplate what he had believed with the brightness of open vision. But when the voice

Rosary Meditations

had been heard over the Son, He was found Himself alone, because when He shall have manifested Himself to His elect, God shall be all in all, yes Christ with His own, as the Head with the body, shall shine through all things."
- St. Bede

The Fifth Luminous Mystery: The Institution of the Eucharist

Scripture References

Matthew 26:26-30; Mark 14:22-25; Luke 22:14-23; John 6:22-59; John 13:1-20; 1 Corinthians 11:23-26

The Story in Brief

On the night before He died, Jesus celebrated the Passover meal with His disciples. At supper, He took bread, blessed it, broke it, and give it to His disciples with the words, "Take, eat; this is My Body." Afterward, He took a cup of wine, gave thanks, and said, "Drink from it, all of you; for this is My Blood of the covenant, which is poured out for many for the forgiveness of sins." He added, "Do this in remembrance of Me."

Points to Ponder

1. Read Matthew 26:17-25, Mark 14:12-21, and Luke 22:7-13, and meditate on how the celebration of Passover became the setting for the First Eucharist. Why did Jesus choose this setting? Consider the Passover symbolism of sacrifice and deliverance, and meditate on Jesus as the new Passover Lamb. You may wish to read and meditate on Scott Hahn's article "The Hunt for the Fourth Cup."[22]

Rosary Meditations

2. Think about the disciples' preparations for the Passover meal. (See Matthew 26:17-19; Mark 14:12-16; and Luke 22:7-13.) Jesus gave His disciples specific instructions, and they found everything just as He said it would be. Try to picture the scene, reflecting especially on the disciples' obedience to Jesus, the title "Teacher," and Jesus' words "My time is near."

3. Just before the meal, Jesus predicted that one of His disciples would betray Him. What kind of atmosphere did this prediction create? Why did Jesus make such a prediction right before the First Eucharist?

4. Jesus blessed the bread first. Why? What is the significance of the bread?

5. Deeply ponder Jesus' words: "Take, eat; this is My Body." and "This is My Body, which is given for you. Do this in remembrance of Me."

6. Jesus broke the sacramental Bread, now His Body, and gave it to the disciples. Meditate on this highest and greatest of self-offerings.

7. Jesus then took the cup and gave thanks (Greek *eucharisteō*).[23] Ponder the significance of wine and of giving thanks.

8. Holding the cup, Jesus said, "Drink from it, all of you; for this is My Blood of the covenant, which is poured out for many for the forgiveness of sins." Reflect carefully on each word.

9. Think closely about the variation of Jesus' words in Luke 22:20: "This cup that is poured out for you is the

The Institution of the Eucharist

new covenant in My Blood." What is the significance of this variation?

10. Meditate on the meaning of "covenant" and on its requirement of complete, self-giving love.

11. Jesus is really present in the Eucharist, Body, Blood, Soul, and Divinity. Ponder this great truth and great mystery.

12. Jesus said that He would not drink from the fruit of the vine again until the day when He would drink it new with the disciples in His Father's Kingdom. What did He mean?

13. In 1 Corinthians 11, Paul recounts the First Eucharist and warns against the abuse of the Sacrament. Paul reminds his readers, "For as often as you eat this bread and drink the cup, you proclaim the Lord's death until He comes." Carefully consider these words.

14. Reflect on Paul's prohibition of eating and drinking the Lord's Body and Blood unworthily; ponder his warning against unbelievers partaking in the Eucharist; and meditate on his call for self-examination before receiving Holy Communion.

15. Why doesn't John's Gospel describe the Institution of the Eucharist?

16. Carefully read and ponder John 6:22-59. Reflect on Jesus as the Bread from heaven and the Bread of life. Meditate on Jesus' words: "Whoever comes to Me will never be hungry, and whoever believes in Me will never be thirsty."

Rosary Meditations

17. How did the Jews' react to Jesus' claims?

18. Think about Jesus' reply to the Jews: "I am the living bread that came down from heaven. Whoever eats of this bread will live forever; and the bread that I will give for the life of the world is My flesh....Very truly, I tell you, unless you eat the flesh of the Son of Man and drink His blood, you have no life in you. Those who eat My flesh and drink My blood have eternal life, and I will raise them up on the last day; for My flesh is true food and My blood is true drink. Those who eat My flesh and drink My blood abide in Me, and I in them. Just as the living Father sent Me, and I live because of the Father, so whoever eats Me will live because of Me..."

19. Jesus' teachings in John 6 were difficult for His listeners to accept. Many of His disciples abandoned Him, but He did not call them back or assure them that He was merely speaking symbolically. He let them go. Reflect on the disciples' disbelief and Jesus' response.

20. Jesus washed the disciples' feet during the Last Supper. Read John 13:1-20, and ponder Jesus' words and actions. Reflect on how this event relates to the Institution of the Eucharist. Think about how Jesus assumed the role of a servant. Also consider Peter's attempt to resist and Jesus' reply to Peter.

21. Take some time to read the sections on the Eucharist in *The Catechism of the Catholic Church*.[24] Also explore the resources available at the *Real Presence Eucharistic Education and Adoration* website.[25] Use this information for further meditation on Jesus' awesome gift of Himself in the Eucharist.

The Institution of the Eucharist

Application Questions

1. Do you believe that Jesus is really and truly present, Body, Blood, Soul, and Divinity, in the Eucharist? How do you live that belief? How does it affect the way in which you receive Jesus in Holy Communion?

2. How are you striving to better understand and appreciate the great gift of the Eucharist?

3. Do you trust in Jesus' words and promises even when they seem impossible or you do not understand them?

4. How do you offer yourself to Jesus?

5. How do you give thanks to God for all that He has given you and especially for the Eucharist?

6. Do you attend Mass on Sundays and Holy Days of Obligation? How do you behave at Mass? Do you give your full attention, or are you distracted? Do you truly understand what happens in the Mass? How might you grow in knowledge, attention, and devotion?

7. Do you receive the Eucharist worthily?

8. How do you prepare your heart to receive Holy Communion? How might you improve your preparation?

9. In what ways are you a servant to other people? How might you grow in your servanthood?

Rosary Meditations

Prayer, Prayer, and More Prayer

Blessing and Adoration – Lord Jesus Christ, we stand in awe of Your total self-offering and great love, and we bow our heads in silent adoration before You, Who are really and truly present, Body, Blood, Soul, and Divinity, in the Eucharist.

Praise – Jesus, we praise You in your awesome greatness and in Your gentle humility. We praise You under the forms of bread and wine. We praise You Who have given Yourself as our food and drink in the Blessed Sacrament.

Thanksgiving – Thank You, Jesus. Thank You for giving us Your very Self, Body, Blood, Soul, and Divinity, in the Holy Eucharist. Thank You for being our Bread of life that has come down from Heaven that we may have eternal life and never be hungry and thirsty again. Thank You for abiding in us and allowing us to abide in You in a very special way when we receive You in Holy Communion.

Intersession – Lord, we lift up to You all those who receive the Eucharist unworthily. Touch their hearts, Lord, and bring them to repentance and to a full and deep belief in Your Real Presence. We lift up to You, too, those Who are not in full communion with the Catholic Church and, therefore, do not have the benefit of receiving You in such an intimate way. Bring them to the fullness of faith, Lord Jesus.

Petition – Jesus, please increase our attention and devotion at Mass, and help us to delve ever deeper into the riches of the Blessed Sacrament. Prevent us from ever receiving You unworthily, and help us to better prepare our hearts to receive You every time we approach You in Holy Communion.

Quotes from the Saints

"The Lord committed His Body and Blood to substances which are formed a homogeneous compound out of many. Bread is made of many grains, wine is produced out of many berries. Herein the Lord Jesus Christ signified us, and hallowed in His own table the mystery of our peace and unity." - St. Augustine

"This bread before the sacramentary words, is the bread in common use; after consecration it is made of bread Christ's flesh. And what are the words, or whose are the phrases of consecration, save those of the Lord Jesus? For if His word had power to make those things begin to be which were not, how much rather will it not be efficacious to cause them to remain what they are, while they are at the same time changed into somewhat else. For if the heavenly word has been effectual in other matters is it ineffectual in heavenly sacraments? Therefore of the bread is made the Body of Christ, and the wine is made blood by the consecration of the heavenly word. Do you inquire after the manner? Learn. The course of nature is, that a man is not born but of man and woman, but by God's will Christ was born of the Holy Spirit and a Virgin." - St. Ambrose

"The Lord invites His servants to set before them Himself for food. But who would dare to eat his Lord; this food when eaten refreshes, but fails not; He lives after being eaten, Who rose again after being put to death. Neither when we eat Him do we divide His substance; but thus it

Rosary Meditations

is in this Sacrament. The faithful know how they feed on Christ's flesh, each man receives a part for himself. He is divided into parts in the Sacrament, yet He remains whole; He is all in heaven, He is all in your heart. They are called Sacraments, because in them what is seen is one thing, what is understood is another, what is seen has a material form, what is understood has spiritual fruit." - St. Augustine

"He gave thanks to instruct us after what manner we ought to celebrate this mystery, and showed also thereby that He came not to His Passion against His will. Also He taught us to bear whatever we suffer with thanksgiving, and infused into us good hopes. For if the type of this sacrifice, to wit, the offering of the paschal lamb, became the deliverance of the people from Egyptian bondage, much more shall the reality thereof be the deliverance of the world. *And gave it to them, saying, Drink you all of it*. That they should not be distressed at hearing this, He first drank His own blood to lead them without fear to the communion of these mysteries." - St. John Chrysostom

"He Himself also breaks the bread, which He gives to His disciples, to show that the breaking of His Body was to take place, not against His will, nor without His intervention; He also blessed it, because He with the Father and the Holy Spirit filled His human nature, which He took upon Him in order to suffer, with the grace of Divine power. He blessed bread and broke it, because He deigned to subject to death His manhood, which He had taken upon Him, in such a way as to show that there was within it the power of Divine immortality, and to teach them that therefore He would the more quickly raise it from the dead. There follows: And gave to them, and said, Take, eat: this is My Body." - St. Bede

The Institution of the Eucharist

"Nor doubt that this is true; for He plainly says, *This is My Body*; but rather receive the words of your Savior in faith. For since He is the Truth, He lies not. They rave foolishly then who say that the mystical blessing loses its power of sanctifying, if any remains are left till the following day. For the most holy Body of Christ will not be changed, but the power of blessing and the life giving grace is ever abiding in it. For the life-giving power of God the Father is the only-begotten Word, which was made flesh not ceasing to be the Word, but making the flesh life giving. What then? Since we have in us the life of God, the Word of God dwelling in us, will our body be life-giving? But it is one thing for us by the habit of participation to have in ourselves the Son of God, another for Himself to have been made flesh, that is, to have made the body which He took from the pure Virgin His own Body. He must needs then be in a certain manner united to our bodies by His holy Body and precious Blood, which we have received for a life giving blessing in the bread and wine. For lest we should be shocked, seeing the Flesh and Blood placed on the holy altars, God, in compassion to our infirmities, pours into the offerings the power of life, changing them into the reality of His own flesh, that the body of life may be found in us, as it were a certain life-giving seed. He adds, *Do this in commemoration of Me.*" - St. Cyril

"It was a thing worthy of Him, Who came from God, and went to God, to trample upon all pride; He rises from supper, and laid aside His garment, and took a towel, and, girded Himself. After that He pours water into a basin, and began to wash His disciples' feet, and to wipe them with the towel wherewith He was girded. See what humility He shows, not only in washing their feet, but in other things. For it was not before, but after they had sat

Rosary Meditations

down, that He rose; and He not only washed them, but laid aside His garments, and girded Himself with a towel, and filled a basin; He did not order others to do all this, but did it Himself, teaching us that we should be willing and ready to do such things." - St. John Chrysostom

Please consult the *Real Presence Eucharistic Education and Adoration Association* website for an abundance of quotations from the saints about the Blessed Sacrament.[26]

The First Sorrowful Mystery: The Agony in the Garden

Scripture References

Matthew 26:36-46; Mark 14:32-42; Luke 22:39-46

The Story in Brief

When Jesus and His disciples had finished the Passover Meal/First Eucharist, they walked out to the Garden of Gethsemane at the foot of the Mount of Olives. Jesus told some of the disciples to wait in a certain place, but He took Peter, James, and John further on with Him. He began to be sorrowful and troubled and asked the three to stay awake while He prayed. Jesus fell to the ground and said, "My Father, if it is possible, let this cup pass from Me; yet not what I want but what You want." When He returned to Peter, James, and John, He found them asleep. After warning them to stay awake and pray that they may not come into the time of trial, He went back to His prayer, saying nearly the same words. Once again, Jesus returned to find His disciples asleep, and once again, He left them and prayed. He was in so much anguish that His sweat became like blood. An angel appeared to Him and gave Him strength. When Jesus returned to the disciples for the last time, He told them to get up, for His betrayer was approaching.

Rosary Meditations

Points to Ponder

1. Consider the setting of this mystery. Gethsemane, which means "oil press," was a garden located at the foot of the Mount of Olives.[27] Jesus and the disciples visited there often. Picture the scene: the darkness, the vegetation, and the isolation.

2. Think about the significance of the garden. Remember that Adam made a choice in the Garden of Eden. Jesus also made a choice in the Garden of Gethsemane. How were their situations similar? How were their choices different?

3. Jesus took His inner circle, Peter, James, and John, with Him. Why these three?

4. Jesus told the disciples, "Sit here while I go over there and pray." Ponder the significance of Jesus' prayer and of prayer in general.

5. Jesus began to be grieved and agitated. Reflect on His very human sorrow. Why was He grieving?

6. The Greek verb for "agitated" is *adēmoneō*.[28] It means to be in anguish, to be troubled, and to be in a great state of anxiety. Picture Jesus in that state, when He was at His most human. No wonder He can understand all our anxiety and distress. Why was Jesus so agitated? Did His human nature recoil at the thought of the cross, or were there other reasons?

7. Jesus said, "I am deeply grieved, even to death; remain here, and stay awake with Me." The word for "I" here is really "My soul," which can mean "Myself" in Greek.[29]

The Agony in the Garden

Think about the identification between the self and the soul that Jesus implied here.

8. Jesus was deeply grieved even to death. This is strong language. Jesus was encompassed with grief and exceedingly sorrowful. He was about to take the weight of the sins of the whole world and all its people of all times onto His shoulders. Mystics have said that, in the garden, Jesus could see all the sins ever committed, all the sins being committed, and all the sins ever to be committed.[30] Meditate on this burden, which may have been even greater than that of the physical cross.

9. Jesus asked the disciples to remain close and stay awake with Him. Why? Did He desire human companionship? Did He want the disciples to understand why He was going to the cross? Did He have more than one motive?

10. Jesus moved a short distance from the disciples, threw Himself on the ground, and began to pray. The Greek words in Matthew's Gospel literally mean "fell on His face." Think about Jesus' humility.

11. Luke says that Jesus knelt down to pray. Why is there a variation in word choice between Luke and the other evangelists? How does Luke's wording capture different aspects of Jesus' act?

12. "My Father, if it is possible, let this cup pass from Me; yet not what I want but what You want." Ponder how these words express the relationship between Jesus and the Father. What was the cup to which Jesus referred? Meditate also on Jesus' self surrender. His human will

Rosary Meditations

was struggling, yet He surrendered to His divine will, which was and is identical to the will of the Father.

13. In Mark's Gospel, Jesus reminded His Father: "...for You all things are possible." God can do all things, but He does not will all things. Meditate on God's will.

14. When Jesus returned to Peter, James, and John, they were sound asleep. Imagine how they must have felt when Jesus caught them.

15. Ponder Jesus' question: "So, could you not stay awake with Me one hour?"

16. Jesus continued, "Stay awake and pray that you may not come into the time of trial..." What was "the time of trial"?

17. What did Jesus mean by "the spirit indeed is willing, but the flesh is weak"?

18. Jesus prayed in nearly the same way a second time: "My Father, if this cannot pass unless I drink it, Your will be done." Meditate on the repetition of prayer. Why did Jesus pray again and again when God certainly heard Him the first time? Why do we often repeat the same prayers? Could prayer be more about changing the one who prays than about changing God?

19. Jesus again returned to the disciples and found them asleep, for their eyes were very heavy. They did not know what to say to Jesus. Luke adds that they were sleeping because of grief. Think about the disciples' state of mind at this point.

The Agony in the Garden

20. Luke tells us that an angel from heaven appeared to Jesus and gave Him strength. Some translations say "comfort," but the Greek word *enischuō* means "to strengthen or invigorate."[31] Why would Jesus need strength from an angel? What kind of strength did the angel give to Jesus?

21. Luke emphasizes the depths of Jesus' agony: "In His anguish He prayed more earnestly, and His sweat became like great drops of blood falling down on the ground." Ponder the intensity of this moment.

22. The Greek word for "agony" can suggest combat. Some mystics describe Jesus as battling with the devil, who was trying to tempt Jesus into abandoning His redemptive mission. These mystics say that the devil was questioning Jesus' identity, purpose, and ability to save the world.[32] Consider this idea.

23. Jesus prayed a third time using the same words and then returned to the disciples, who were asleep yet again. Jesus asked them, "Are you still sleeping and taking your rest?" How come the disciples still could not stay awake, even after being scolded by Jesus twice before?

24. Jesus continued, "See, the hour is at hand, and the Son of Man is betrayed into the hands of sinners. Get up, let us be going. See My betrayer is at hand." What did He mean by "the hour"? Jesus knew what was going to happen to Him, and He went out to meet it. He had prayed, and He was now prepared. His betrayer, Judas, was close by.

Rosary Meditations

Application Questions

1. What choices are you making in your life? What choices have you made in the past? Are your choices more like Jesus' or more like Adam's?

2. How often and in what ways do you pray?

3. When you are in a state of grace, you are a member of Jesus' "inner circle"; how would a constant recollection of this fact change your life?

4. Do you turn to God when you are sorrowful, troubled, and in anguish? What do you say to Him? How have you felt His presence during these times?

5. Do you realize how much sorrow your sins bring to Jesus? How would such a realization make you less likely to commit sin?

6. Are you attentive during prayer, or do you get distracted? How might you limit your distractions during prayer?

7. What do you believe about the nature and purpose of prayer?

8. How does your prayer change you?

9. Is it difficult for you to imitate Jesus and say to God "yet not what I want, but what You want"? Why or why not?

10. How do you accept God's will when it is not your will?

The Agony in the Garden

11. Can you stay awake with Jesus for one hour? What does staying awake with Jesus mean to you?

12. Have there been times when you are "sleepy" in your spiritual life? What are these times like? How do you overcome them?

13. How do you handle the trials in your life?

14. When has your spirit been willing but your flesh weak?

15. Do you have a relationship with the angels? How do the angels influence your life?

16. How have you struggled with the devil? Do you rely on Jesus to strengthen you?

Prayer, Prayer, and More Prayer

Blessing and Adoration – Dearest Jesus, You sweated blood for us in the garden. You suffered tremendous anguish because of our sins. We bow our heads in silent adoration, Lord, as we recognize Your unwavering, unending love for us.

Praise – We praise you, Jesus, for Your courage. Even though You are God, You are still Man, and as a Man, you had to battle with the devil. But You won! You conquered him in the garden; You conquered him on the cross; and You saved us from his clutches. We praise You, victorious Jesus.

Thanksgiving – Jesus, we thank You for showing us that You can and do understand all our trials, both physical and mental. In the garden, You experienced extreme distress and sorrow. We thank You for accepting Your Father's will, even in the face of that pain, and for choosing to go to the cross for our salvation.

Intercession – Jesus, we lift up to You all people who are experiencing fear, grief, sorrow, distress, and affliction. Hold them close to You, Lord, and calm their hearts. Wrap them in a warm blanket of Your love that they may feel and know Your understanding, gentle care.

Petition – Jesus, please give us strength in our hours of fear and anguish. Inspire us to turn to prayer when we are in need and always to surrender to Your will when we must drink from the cup of suffering.

Quotes from the Saints

"But seeing that prayer is the sending up [of] the understanding to God, or the asking of God [for] things fitting, how did the Lord pray? For His understanding needed not to be lifted up to God, having been once united hypostatically to God the Word. Neither could He need to ask of God things fitting, for the One Christ is both God and Man. But giving in Himself a pattern to us, He taught us to ask of God, and to lift up our minds to Him. As He took on Him our passions, that by triumphing over them Himself, He might give us also the victory over them, so now He prays to open to us the way to that lifting up to God, to fulfill for us all righteousness, to reconcile His Father to us, to pay honor to Him as the First Cause, and to show that He is not against God." - St. John Damascene

The Agony in the Garden

"I suppose that there are some who offer here no other cause of His fear than His passion and death. I ask those who think thus, whether it stands with reason that He should have feared to die, Who banished from the Apostles all fear of death, and exhorted them to the glory of martyrdom? How can we suppose Him to have felt pain and grief in the sacrament of death, Who rewards with life those who die for Him? And what pangs of death could He fear, Who came to death of the free choice of His own power? And if His Passion was to do Him honor, how could the fear of His Passion make Him sorrowful?" - St. Hilary

"Our Lord therefore sorrowed to prove the reality of the Man which He had taken upon Him…" - St. Jerome

"He is sorrowful, yet not Himself, but His soul; not His Wisdom, not His divine Substance, but His soul, for He took upon Him my soul, and my body." - St. Ambrose

"As being God, dwelling in the body, He shows the frailty of flesh, that the blasphemy of those who deny the mystery of His Incarnation might find no place; for having taken up a body, He must needs also take up all that belongs to the body, hunger, thirst, pain, grief; for the Godhead cannot suffer the changes of these affections. - St. Bede

"But what means His bending of knees? Of which it is said, *And He kneeled down, and prayed.* It is the way of men to pray to their superiors with their faces on the ground, testifying by the action that the greater of the two are those who are asked. Now it is plain that human nature contains nothing worthy of God's imitation. Accordingly the tokens of respect which we evince to one

Rosary Meditations

another, confessing ourselves to be inferior to our neighbors, we have transferred to the humiliation of the Incomparable Nature. And thus He who bore our sicknesses and interceded for us, bent His knee in prayer, by reason of the man which He assumed, giving us an example, that we ought not to exalt ourselves at the time of prayer, but in all things be conformed to humility; *for God resists the proud, but gives grace to the humble.*" - St. Gregory of Nyssa

"It is indeed impossible for the soul of man not to be tempted. Therefore He says not, Pray that you be not tempted, but, *Pray that you enter not into temptation*, that is, that the temptation [does] not at last overcome you." - St. Bede

"There were, I conclude, two ways in which this cup of Passion might pass from the Lord. If He should drink it, it would pass away from Him, and afterwards from the whole race of mankind also; if He should not drink it, it would perhaps pass from Him, but from men it would not pass. He would fain therefore that it should so pass from Him as that He should not at all taste its bitterness, yet only if it were possible, saving the righteousness of God. If it were not possible, He was rather willing to drink it, that so it might pass from Him, and from the whole race of mankind rather than against His Father's will shun the drinking thereof." - Origen

"That by His second prayer He might show Himself to be very man. It goes on: *And when He returned, He found them asleep again*; He however did not rebuke them severely. For their eyes were heavy, (that is, with sleep,) neither wist they what to answer Him. By this learn the weakness of men, and let us not, whom even sleep can

The Agony in the Garden

overcome, promise things which are impossible to us. Therefore He goes away the third time to pray the prayer mentioned above." - Theophylact

"Having concluded His third prayer, and having obtained that the Apostles' terror should be corrected by subsequent penitence, He goes forth undaunted by the prospect of His own Passion to meet His pursuers, and offers Himself voluntarily to be sacrificed. *Arise, let us be going*; as much as to say, Let them not find you trembling, let us go forth willingly to death, that they may see us confident and rejoicing in suffering; *Lo, he that shall betray Me draws near.*" - St. Jerome

"But He prays, that the cup may pass away, to show that He is very man, wherefore He adds: *Take away this cup from Me*. But remembering why He was sent, He accomplishes the dispensation for which He was sent, and cries out, *But not what I will, but what You will*. As if He had said, If death can die, without My dying according to the flesh, let this cup pass away; but since this cannot be otherwise, not what I will, but what You will. Many still are sad at the prospect of death, but let them keep their heart right, and avoid death as much as they can; but if they cannot, then let them say what the Lord said for us. - St. Bede

"Now every art is set forth by the words and works of him who teaches it. Because then our Lord had come to teach no ordinary virtue, therefore He speaks and does the same things. And so having in words commanded to pray, lest they enter into temptation, He does the same likewise in work, saying, *Father, if You be willing, remove this cup from Me*. He said not the words, If You will, as if ignorant whether it was pleasing to the Father. For such

Rosary Meditations

knowledge was not more difficult than the knowledge of His Father's substance, which He alone clearly knew, according to John, *As the Father knows Me, even so have I known the Father*. Nor says He this, as refusing His Passion. For He who rebuked a disciple, who wished to prevent His Passion, so as even after many commendations, to call him Satan, how should He be unwilling to be crucified? Consider then why it was so said. How great a thing was it to hear that the unspeakable God, Who passes all understanding, was content to enter the virgin's womb, to suck her milk, and to undergo every thing human. Since then that was almost incredible which was about to happen, He sent first indeed Prophets to announce it, afterwards He Himself comes clothed in the flesh, so that you could not suppose Him to be a phantom. He permits His flesh to endure all natural infirmities, to hunger, to thirst, to sleep, to labor, to be afflicted, to be tormented; on this account likewise He refuses not death, that He might manifest thereby His true humanity." - St. John Chrysostom

"Many are shocked at this place who turn the sorrows of the Savior to an argument of inherent weakness from the beginning, rather than taken upon Him for the time. But I am so far from considering it a thing to be excused, that I never more admire His mercy and majesty; for He would have conferred less upon me had He not taken upon Him my feelings. For He took upon Him my sorrow, that upon me He might bestow His joy. With confidence therefore I name His sadness, because I preach His cross. He must needs then have undergone affliction, that He might conquer. For they have no praise of fortitude whose wounds have produced stupor rather than pain. He wished therefore to instruct us how we should conquer death, and what is far greater, the anguish of coming death. You smarted then, O Lord, not from Your own but my wounds; for *He was wounded for our transgressions*. And perhaps He is sad, because that after Adam's fall the passage by which we must depart from this world was such that death was necessary. Nor is it far from the truth that He was sad for His persecutors, who He knew would suffer punishment for their wicked sacrilege." - St. Ambrose

Rosary Meditations

The Second Sorrowful Mystery: The Scourging at the Pillar

Scripture References

Matthew 27:26; Mark 15:15; Luke 23:16, 22; John 19:1

The Story in Brief

Judas led an armed crowd to the Garden of Gethsemane to arrest Jesus, Who then appeared as a prisoner before the high priest and council, before Herod, and before Pontius Pilate. Peter, who was standing in the courtyard waiting to hear the results of the trials, denied Jesus three times, exactly as He had predicted. The Jews called for Jesus' crucifixion, but Pilate was unwilling. He offered to release Jesus according to the custom of the Jewish feast, but the Jews chose Barabbas instead and continued to insist that Jesus be crucified. Pilate finally gave in, symbolically washed his hands of the matter, and turned Jesus over to the Roman soldiers to be scourged and executed.

Points to Ponder

1. Because Matthew, Mark, and John devote only one verse each to the scourging at the pillar and Luke offers only two brief references, you may wish to spend some time meditating on the events leading up to the

Rosary Meditations

scourging. Carefully read Matthew 26:47–27:26, Mark 14:43–15:15, Luke 22:47–23:25, and John 18:1–19:6, and ponder some of the points below.

2. Think about the scene of Jesus' betrayal. Consider some the following:
- The crowd coming to arrest Jesus with swords and clubs
- Judas' betraying kiss
- Jesus' response: "Friend, do what you are here to do."
- The crowd's reaction when Jesus said, "I AM"
- The meaning of "I AM"
- The altercation between Peter and the high priest's servant
- Jesus healing the servant's ear
- Jesus' acceptance of His arrest so that the "Scriptures be fulfilled"
- The disciples' desertion

3. Meditate on Jesus' trial before the high priest and council. Ponder these points:
- The false testimony against Jesus
- Jesus' silence in the face of the Jews' accusations
- Jesus' testimony: "From now on you will see the Son of Man seated at the right hand of Power and coming on the clouds of heaven."
- The high priest's verdict
- The abuse Jesus received at the hands of the Jews

4. Reflect on Peter's denial of Jesus. Consider the reasons for the denial; Jesus' prediction and response; Peter's violent outburst; and Peter's remorse.

The Scourging at the Pillar

5. Think about Jesus' trial before Pilate. Mediate on a few of the following:
- The Jews' accusations
- Pilate's questions to Jesus, especially "Are You the King of the Jews?" and "What is truth?"
- Jesus' silence before His accusers
- Pilate's wife's dream and her proclamation of Jesus' innocence
- Jesus' words to Pilate about the Kingdom: "My Kingdom is not from here."
- The Jews' choice to release Barabbas
- Pilate's fear
- Pilate's verdict of "not guilty"
- Pilate caving in to the Jews when they implied that if he released Jesus, he would be betraying Caesar
- The Jews' claim that they had no king but Caesar and their cries to crucify Jesus
- Pilate washing his hands of the matter and declaring himself innocent of Jesus' blood

6. Reflect on Jesus' trial before Herod in Luke's Gospel. Why does Luke include this scene? Think about Jesus' silence; the mockery and abuse He endured; and how Herod sent Him back to Pilate dressed in an elegant robe.

7. Ponder the actual scourging of Jesus. Roman soldiers lashed Him repeatedly with a whip that probably had at least two "tails" tipped with metal balls. The Jews limited their scourgings to thirty-nine lashes, but the Romans did not. For more detailed information about the scourging, see *The Crucifixion* website.[33] Please be warned; it contains disturbing material.

Rosary Meditations

8. Reflect on Jesus' extreme pain, and remember that He suffered that pain because of our sins.

9. Consider how strong Jesus' love was. He loved His tormentors even as they scourged Him, and He loves us even when we sin.

10. Is there any pain that Jesus cannot understand?

11. Remember that Jesus could have stopped the scourging, and the entire Passion, at any point. He was and is God. But He chose to suffer all for our sake, to save us, to bring us home to Heaven to be with Him forever. Ponder this amazing truth.

12. Place yourself in the sandals of those who witnessed the scourging. What did they see? How did they react?

Application Questions

1. How have you betrayed Jesus? Have you repented of your sins and confessed them? Do you understand that Jesus forgives you and loves you even when you do betray Him?

2. How do you respond when you are falsely accused by someone?

3. In what ways have you, like Peter, denied Jesus? How did you feel afterward?

4. Have you ever been influenced to do something you knew was wrong? Have you ever followed the crowd instead of your conscience? Why did you do so? How did you feel afterward?

The Scourging at the Pillar

5. Do you truly realize and understand what Jesus endured for you?

6. How should you respond to Jesus' self-giving love?

7. Do you realize that Jesus completely understands your pain? How might this realization change your relationship with Him and your perspective on the sufferings in your own life?

Prayer, Prayer, and More Prayer

Blessing and Adoration – We bow our heads in silent adoration before You, our suffering Jesus. We adore You, and we bless You, for You suffered unspeakable pain and anguish for our sake. How can we ever truly grasp Your wondrous love for us?

Praise – Jesus, we praise You for Your great courage and love. You stood silently before Your accusers and allowed Yourself to be abused and scourged. You could have stopped it all at any moment, but You chose to continue out of love for us. May Your praises ring out in Heaven and earth, Lord Jesus!

Thanksgiving – Lord, how can we ever thank You enough? You were betrayed, denied, and abused by the ones You love. You suffered for us. You bore the pain and anguish of our sins. And You did it all willingly that we may be with You in Heaven forever.

Intercession – Lord, we lift up to You all those in pain. Comfort them and strengthen them. We lift up those who even today do not recognize You as the divine Son. Touch their hearts that they may know You. We lift up those

Rosary Meditations

who are tempted to bow to the will of the crowd instead of following their consciences. Give them courage. We lift up those who are physically abused. Hold them closely in Your arms and protect them. We lift up their abusers. Change their hearts and their ways.

Petition – Jesus, help us always to remember that no matter what we must suffer, You are always there beside us, and You understand fully what we are going through. Help us to turn to You for strength, courage, and self-control. Forgive us our sins, Lord, as we fall before You in sorrow and repentance.

Quotes from the Saints

"It should be known that Pilate administered the Roman law, which enacted that every one who was crucified should first be scourged. Jesus then is given up to the soldiers to be beaten, and they tore with whips that most holy body and capacious bosom of God. This was done that we might be delivered from those stripes of which it is said, *Many stripes shall be to the wicked.*" - St. Jerome

"See the Lord is made ready for the scourge, see now it descends upon Him! That sacred skin is torn by the fury of the rods; the cruel might of repeated blows lacerates His shoulders. Ah me! God is stretched out before man, and He, in Whom not one trace of sin can be discerned, suffers punishment as a malefactor." - St. John Chrysostom

"When the Jews had cried out that they did not wish Jesus to be released on account of the passover, but Barabbas. Then Pilate therefore took Jesus, and scourged Him. Pilate seems to have done this for no reason but to

The Scourging at the Pillar

satisfy the malice of the Jews with some punishment short of death. On which account he allowed his band to do what follows, or perhaps even commanded them." - St. Augustine

Rosary Meditations

The Third Sorrowful Mystery: The Crowning of Thorns

Scripture References

Matthew 27:27-31; Mark 15:16-20; John 19:2-5

The Story in Brief

Before Jesus was crucified, the Roman soldiers decided to have a bit of "fun" at His expense. They gathered around Him, stripped Him, and clothed Him in a reddish purple robe. They made a crown of thorns and forced it onto His head. Then they put a reed in His right hand. They knelt before Him in mockery, saying "Hail, King of the Jews!" They spat on Him and struck Him. When they had finished, they dressed Him in His own clothes and led Him away to be crucified.

Points to Ponder

1. Before the Roman soldiers crucified Jesus, they tortured Him by crowning Him with thorns and mocking Him as "King of the Jews!" Why would the soldiers do such a thing?

2. Matthew and Mark say that the soldiers gathered the whole cohort around Jesus. Try to picture the various

soldiers. Do you think they all participated in this cruel mockery? Or were some appalled by it?

3. The soldiers stripped Jesus. Remember that He was badly wounded from the scourging. Consider His pain as His wounds were torn open.

4. Think about the humiliation Jesus suffered when He was forcibly stripped. Recall that He could have stopped everything at any point, but He chose not to. Why?

5. The soldiers dressed Jesus in a robe. Matthew tells us that it was scarlet while Mark and John describe it as purple. The Greek words used by Mark and John both refer to a reddish purple that could easily resemble a faded scarlet.[34] Ponder the significance of these colors. Why would Matthew tell us that the robe was scarlet? What does the color scarlet make you think of? Why would Mark and John choose a different focus and identify the color as purple? What does purple signify? Recall that purple dye was generally quite expensive and used for clothing for the elite classes.

6. Ponder the crown of thorns. The thorns the soldiers used were not the small thorns we find on roses. They were long, tough, and sharp. Some authors have suggested that the soldiers may have pushed the thorns through an old basket and pressed that onto Jesus' head.[35] In any case, these thorns would have caused Jesus great agony as they were forced into His scalp.

7. The soldiers placed a reed in Jesus' right hand. Why did they do so?

The Crowning of Thorns

8. The soldiers then mocked Jesus, kneeling before Him in false veneration and proclaiming "Hail, King of the Jews!" Picture the scene. Reflect on how much this mockery must have hurt Jesus. He loved these men, and He had come to save them.

9. Consider the irony here. Jesus is a King, the King of the entire universe. The mocking soldiers did not know that. They did not realize that they should have been falling on their faces before Jesus in true adoration. Instead, they laughed at their cruel jokes.

10. The soldiers went beyond nasty words and false bows. They spat on Jesus. They snatched the reed from His hand and hit Him on the head with it. What is your response to this kind of violence?

11. After the soldiers had tired of their abhorrent game, they stripped Jesus of the reddish purple robe and dressed Him in His own clothes. Then they led Him away to be crucified. Ponder this scene.

12. In John's Gospel, Pilate presented Jesus to the crowd one more time while He was still wearing the crown of thorns and the robe. This is not contradictory to the other Gospels; John simply chose to include an event that the others, for whatever reason, do not mention. The crowds rejected Jesus and called for His crucifixion. Meditate on Pilate's actions, Jesus' appearance, and the crowd's response.

13. What does the crowning of thorns reveal to us about Jesus? Consider His silence in the face of the soldiers' cruel mockery and physical abuse.

Rosary Meditations

Application Questions

1. Have you ever seen or been part of a crowd that was being cruel to another person? How did that cruelty make you feel? Did you do anything to stop it? Why or why not?

2. Have you ever been abused and mocked? How did you respond? Where did you turn for help?

3. Is Jesus Christ the king of your life? Why or why not? What difference does it make in your life when Jesus is in command?

4. Do people or things sometimes take Jesus' place as king of your life? What are they? Why do they take precedence over Jesus? How might you put these people or things in their proper positions?

5. Is there any mental or physical pain that Jesus cannot understand? Do you bring your mental and physical pain to Jesus? When you do so, is that pain easier to bear? How so?

6. Do you value silence in the face of abuse? Why or why not?

Prayer, Prayer, and More Prayer

Blessing and Adoration – Jesus, we bow our heads in silent adoration as we contemplate You wearing the crown of thorns and the robe of mockery. We know that You could have stopped the whole thing at any moment, but You did not because You were doing it all for us. We love You, Jesus.

The Crowning of Thorns

Praise – We praise You, Jesus, for Your great courage, patience, and love in the face of such cruelty as You experienced during the crowning of thorns. We praise You for loving us so much that You willingly suffered this kind of brutality.

Thanksgiving – Lord, we can never thank You enough for what You have done to save us. You experienced pain beyond telling, both physical and emotional, but You never complained. You love us that much.

Intercession – Jesus, we lift up to You all those who are experiencing physical and/or mental abuse. Please wrap them up in Your love, comfort them, and give them strength. We lift up their abusers. Touch their hearts, Lord, and change them. We lift up those who are too afraid to stand up when they see others being mocked and abused. Fill them with courage, Lord, so they may do what they know is right.

Petition – Jesus, please give us the strength to bear all our sufferings and to unite our pain with Yours. Please help us to imitate You when we are mocked and abused and not lash out at our abusers but continue to love them and pray for them.

Quotes from the Saints

"He had been styled King of the Jews, and the Scribes and Priests had brought this charge against Him, that He claimed sovereignty over the Jewish nation; hence this mockery of the soldiers, taking away His own garments, they put on Him a scarlet cloak to represent that purple fringe which kings of old used to wear, for the diadem they put on Him a crown of thorns, and for the regal

Rosary Meditations

scepter give Him a reed, and perform adoration to Him as to a king." - St. Jerome

"What should we henceforth care if any one insults us, after Christ has thus suffered? The utmost that cruel outrage could do was put in practice against Christ; and not one member only, but His whole body suffered injuries; His head from the crown, the reed, and the buffetings; His face which was spit upon; His cheeks which they smote with the palms of their hands; His whole body from the scourging, the stripping to put on the cloak, and the mockery of homage; His hands from the reed which they put into them in mimicry of a scepter; as though they were afraid of omitting aught of indignity." - St. John Chrysostom

"The Lord having taken upon Him all the infirmities of our body, is then covered with the scarlet colored blood of all the martyrs, to whom is due the Kingdom with Him; He is crowned with thorns, that is, with the sins of the Gentiles who once pierced Him, for there is a prick in thorns of which is woven the crown of victory for Christ. In the reed, He takes into His hand and supports the weakness and frailty of the Gentiles; and His head is smitten therewith that the weakness of the Gentiles sustained by Christ's hand may rest on God the Father, who is His head." - St. Hilary

"But instead of the diadem, they put on Him a crown of thorns, wherefore it goes on, *And platted a crown of thorns, and put it about His head.* And for a royal scepter they give Him a reed, as Matthew writes, and they bow before Him as a king, wherefore there follows, *And began to salute Him, Hail, King of the Jews!* And that the soldiers worshiped Him as one who falsely called Himself

The Crowning of Thorns

God, is clear from what is added: *And bowing their knees, worshiped Him*, as though He pretended to be God." - St. Bede

"For instead of a diadem, they put upon Him a crown of thorns, and a purple robe to represent the purple robe which kings wear. Matthew says, *a scarlet robe*, but scarlet and purple are different names for the same color. And though the soldiers did this in mockery, yet to us their acts have a meaning. For by the crown of thorns is signified the taking of our sins upon Him, the thorns which the earth of our body brings forth. And the purple robe signifies the flesh crucified. For our Lord is robed in purple, wherever He is glorified by the triumphs of holy martyrs." - St. Bede

Rosary Meditations

The Fourth Sorrowful Mystery: The Carrying of the Cross

Scripture References

Matthew 27:32; Mark 15:21; Luke 23:26-31; John 19:17

The Story in Brief

When the soldiers led Jesus out to be crucified on Calvary, they made Him carry His cross. He had been so badly wounded and was so exhausted that He fell three times along the way. The soldiers compelled Simon of Cyrene to help Jesus so He would not die before He reached the scene of crucifixion. Along the way, Jesus met His mother, Mary. He also encountered Veronica, who compassionately wiped His bloody, sweaty face and afterward discovered that He had left His own holy image on the cloth she had used. Later, He spoke with some women of Jerusalem who were lamenting His fate. Finally, Jesus reached Calvary. He was about to die for our sins.

Points to Ponder

1. The Biblical account of Jesus carrying His cross is very brief, but the Church's Tradition offers us further details and insights in the Stations of the Cross. Take a few

Rosary Meditations

minutes to examine some Stations of the Cross websites or booklets,[36] and ponder a few of the following points.

2. Matthew, Mark, and Luke tell us that the Roman soldiers compelled Simon of Cyrene to carry Jesus' cross. John, on the other hand, emphasizes that Jesus carried the cross Himself. Both these statements can be true if we think about how weak Jesus would have been during His walk to Calvary. He may have started out carrying His cross by Himself and later required assistance from Simon. Picture Jesus carrying His cross. Remember how badly wounded He already was from the scourging and crowning of thorns.

3. What was Simon of Cyrene's response when he was forced to carry the cross with Jesus?

4. Mark mentions that Simon was the father of Alexander and Rufus. This reference suggests that Simon's sons were probably Christians and well known in the early Christian community. Ponder the significance of this.

5. The Stations of the Cross tell us that Jesus fell once before Simon of Cyrene was pressed into service. Reflect on Jesus' pain and weakness as He fell to the ground beneath the heavy cross.

6. Jesus met His mother, Mary, as He walked toward Calvary. Meditate on this encounter. Picture the expressions on the faces of the Son and the mother. Imagine what they might have said to one another. What was Mary feeling as she saw her Son's pain? What was Jesus feeling as He gazed on His mother's face?

The Carrying of the Cross

7. Consider the behavior of the crowd that lined the streets. Imagine the range of responses the Jews and Romans exhibited as they watched Jesus walk the way of the cross. Some probably abused Him as a criminal. Others may have felt sorry for Him. Were His followers mixed in with the crowd? What were they thinking when they saw Jesus?

8. According to the Stations of the Cross, a woman named Veronica wiped Jesus' bloody, sweaty face with a cloth. Imagine Jesus' Holy Face. Consider Veronica's courage as she flaunted the Roman soldiers to approach Jesus and minister to Him.

9. When Veronica looked at the cloth she had used to wipe the Lord's face, she discovered an image of Jesus. What a reward for her kindness and care! Try to picture the image on Veronica's cloth. What did it look like?

10. Also note that the name "Veronica" means "true icon." Veronica received her new name after she had discovered Jesus' image. Reflect on how that event became the defining moment of her life.

11. Jesus fell a second time, but He got up again and kept going despite His pain. Ponder His courage.

12. Luke tells us that some women were in the crowd, beating their breasts and wailing for Jesus. They were clearly distressed at seeing Him so mistreated. Reflect on their thoughts and actions.

13. Read Jesus' response to the women in Luke 23:28-31. His words were mysterious, suggesting a time of trial and probably pointing to more than one future event,

Rosary Meditations

including the fall of Jerusalem in 70 A.D. and perhaps even the end times. Meditate on Jesus' words.

14. Jesus fell once again as He neared Calvary. By this time, He would have been exhausted, but He got up and continued on His path to the cross. Ponder Jesus' complete self-surrender.

15. Walk with Jesus along the way of the cross. Place yourself next to Him and journey with Him on the road to Calvary.

Application Questions

1. How do you take up your cross and follow Jesus? What are the crosses in your life? How do you respond to them? Do you join your personal way of the cross to that of Jesus? How might your life be different if you did so more often?

2. Are there any sins that you need to confess? Which particular sins do you struggle with the most? Do you take them to Jesus and ask for help? Why or why not?

3. When have you fallen, physically and/or spiritually, in your life? What does it feel like to fall? When you fall, do you get up and keep going? Why or why not?

4. Do you share your pain with others? Do others share their pain with you? What are those experiences like? How do you help other people carry their crosses? How do you comfort those who are in pain?

The Carrying of the Cross

5. How would you have behaved if you had been part of the crowd that was watching Jesus as He carried His cross to Calvary?

6. What are the defining moments in your spiritual life?

7. Are you a courageous person? Why or why not?

8. Do you ever weep for the world and for the people around you? Why? How do you intercede for others in prayer?

9. Have you surrendered you entire life, your entire self, to God? If not, will you do so? How would such a surrender change your life?

Prayer, Prayer, and More Prayer

Blessing and Adoration – Lord Jesus, we bow before You in silent adoration as we contemplate Your way of the cross. We adore You as we watch You struggle in pain and exhaustion. You did it all for us that we might be with You in Heaven forever. We love You, Jesus.

Praise – We praise You, Jesus, for Your courage. We praise You for surrendering Your entire Self to the Father. We praise You for carrying Your cross for us. We praise You for Your tremendous love.

Thanksgiving – Lord, You suffered unspeakable pain and anguish for us when You carried the cross. You taught us how to carry our own crosses, and You walk right along with us when we must. How can we ever thank You enough?

Rosary Meditations

Intercession – Jesus, we lift up to You all those who must carry their crosses. We lift up those who are in pain. We lift up those who must stand beside the suffering and comfort them. We lift up those who mourn. Hold them all in You loving arms, Lord.

Petition – Jesus, please accompany us as we carry our crosses. Please give us courage and perseverance, and never leave us alone. Please give us compassion for those who are suffering that we may comfort them and help them carry their crosses.

Quotes from the Saints

"...as they went out, they laid hold of Simon, but when they drew near to the place in which they would crucify Him, they laid the cross upon Him that He might bear it. Simon obtained not this office by chance, but was brought to the spot by God's providence, that he might be found worthy of mention in the Scriptures of the Gospel, and of the ministry of the cross of Christ. And it was not only meet that the Savior should carry His cross, but meet also that we should take part therein, filling a carriage so beneficial to us. Yet would it not have so profited us to take it on us, as we have profited by His taking it upon Himself." - Origen

"...since this Simon is not called a man of Jerusalem, but a Cyrenian, (for Cyrene is a city of Libya,) fitly is he taken to mean the nations of the Gentiles, which were once foreigners and strangers to the covenants, but now by obedience are heirs of God, and joint heirs with Christ. Whence also Simon is fitly interpreted 'obedient,' and Cyrene 'an heir.' But he is said to come from a country place, for a country place is called 'pagos' in Greek,

The Carrying of the Cross

wherefore those whom we see to be aliens from the city of God, we call pagans. Simon then coming out from the country carries the cross after Jesus, when the Gentile nations leaving pagan rites embrace obediently the footsteps of our Lord's Passion." - St. Bede

"For no one else accepted to bear the cross, because the wood was counted an abomination. Accordingly upon Simon the Cyrenian they imposed as it were to his dishonor the bearing of the cross, which others refused. Here is fulfilled that prophecy of Isaiah, *Whose government shall be upon his shoulder*. For the government of Christ is His cross; for which the Apostle says, *God has exalted Him*. And as for a mark of dignity, some wear a belt, others a head dress, so our Lord the cross. And if you seek, you will find that Christ does not reign in us save by hardships, whence it comes that the luxurious are the enemies of the cross of Christ." - Theophylact

"Christ therefore bearing His cross, already as a conqueror carried his trophies. The cross is laid upon His shoulders, because whether Simon or Himself bore it, both Christ bore it in the man, and the man in Christ. Nor do the accounts of the Evangelists differ, since the mystery reconciles them. And it is the rightful order of our advance that Christ should first Himself erect the trophy of His cross, then hand it down to be raised by His martyrs. He is not a Jew who bears the cross, but an alien and a foreigner, nor does he precede but follow, according as it is written, *Let him take up his cross, and follow Me*." - St. Ambrose

"A large multitude indeed followed the cross of Christ, but with very different feelings. For the people who had demanded His death were rejoicing that they should see Him dying, the women weeping that He was about to die. But He was followed by the weeping only of women. Not because that vast crowd of men was not also sorrowful at His Passion, but because the less esteemed female sex could more freely give utterance to what they thought." - St. Bede

"By *these days* He signifies the time of the siege and captivity which was coming upon them from the Romans, of which He had said before, *Woe to them that are with child, and give suck in those days.* It is natural, when captivity by an enemy is threatening, to seek for refuge in fastnesses or hidden places, where men may lie concealed. And so it follows, *Then shall they begin to say to the mountains, Fall on us; and to the hills, Cover us.* For Josephus relates, that when the Romans pressed hard upon them, the Jews sought hastily the caverns of the mountains, and the lurking places in the hills. It may be also that the words, *Blessed are the barren,* are to be understood of those of both sexes, who have made themselves eunuchs for the Kingdom of Heaven's sake, and that it is said to the mountains and hills, *Fall upon us, and Cover us,* because all who are mindful of their own weakness, when the crisis of their temptations breaks upon them, have sought to be protected by the example, precept, and prayers, of certain high and saintly men." - St. Bede

"They compel Jesus to bear the cross, regarding it as unholy, and therefore avoiding the touch of it themselves. And He bearing His cross went forth into a place called the place of a skull, which is called in Hebrew Golgotha, where they crucified Him. The same was done typically by Isaac, who carried the wood. But then the matter only proceeded as far as his father's good pleasure ordered, but now it was fully accomplished, for the reality had appeared." - St. John Chrysostom

"Great spectacle, to the profane a laughing-stock, to the pious a mystery. Profaneness sees a King bearing a cross instead of a scepter; piety sees a King bearing a cross, thereon to nail Himself, and afterwards to nail it on the foreheads of kings. That to profane eyes was contemptible, which the hearts of Saints would afterwards glory in; Christ displaying His own cross on His shoulders, and bearing that which was not to be put under a bushel, the candlestick of that candle which was now about to burn." - St. Augustine

"He carried the badge of victory on His shoulders, as conquerors do. Some say that the place of Calvary was where Adam died and was buried; so that in the very place on where death reigned, there Jesus erected His trophy." - St. John Chrysostom

Rosary Meditations

The Fifth Sorrowful Mystery: The Crucifixion

Scripture References

Matthew 27:33-56; Mark 15:22-40; Luke 23:32-49; John 19:17-37

The Story in Brief

Jesus was crucified on Calvary or, in Hebrew, Golgotha. The soldiers stripped Him, nailed Him to the cross, and lifted Him up to die a slow, excruciating death by suffocation. They cast lots to divide His clothes, particularly His seamless tunic. Pontius Pilate ordered a sign placed above Jesus' head: "Jesus of Nazareth, King of the Jews." Jesus was crucified between two criminals. At first, they joined the crowd in taunting Him, but then one of them had a change of heart. He admitted his crimes and testified to Jesus' innocence. "Jesus, remember me when You come into Your Kingdom," he begged. Jesus' mother, St. John, and several women stood near the cross. When Jesus saw His mother and St. John, He said to Mary, "Woman, behold your son." He said to St. John, "Behold your mother." As Jesus approached His death, He cried out, "Eli, Eli lema sacbachthani" and said, "I am thirsty." After He had taken a little wine, He cried out in a loud voice, "It is finished!" Then He gave up His Spirit. A nearby soldier

Rosary Meditations

pierced Jesus' side with a lance, and blood and water flowed out. The soldier loudly proclaimed Jesus' innocence, even going so far as to call Him the Son of God. Joseph of Arimathea claimed Jesus' body and buried Him in a new tomb.

Points to Ponder

1. Jesus was crucified on Calvary or Golgotha, which means "The Place of the Skull" in Hebrew. Meditate on the name Golgotha.

2. Ponder the fact that the place of Jesus' crucifixion was near the traditional site of Abraham's near-sacrifice of Isaac in Genesis 22.[37]

3. Golgotha was outside the city gates. What does this symbolize?

4. When Jesus arrived at Calvary, He was offered wine mixed with bitter gall and/or myrrh to drink. The Jews had a custom of offering such a mixture to someone about to be crucified because it would intoxicate the person and help dull the pain of crucifixion.[38] Jesus tasted the wine but refused to drink it. Why? What does this refusal tell us about Jesus?

5. The soldiers nailed Jesus to the cross. Then they elevated the cross and left Him to hang there, dying a slow, painful death by suffocation. Ponder Jesus' agony.

6. Reflect on why Jesus freely suffered such agony.

7. When the soldiers cast lots to divide Jesus' clothes, they fulfilled the prophecy of Psalm 22:8. Jesus was

The Crucifixion

wearing a seamless tunic that had been woven in one piece, and the soldiers did not wish to tear it. Picture the soldiers as they divided up Jesus' clothing. Also meditate on the symbolism of the seamless garment.

8. Pontius Pilate ordered an inscription to be hung over Jesus' head that read, "Jesus of Nazareth, King of the Jews" in Hebrew, Latin, and Greek, the languages of the known world at the time. The Jews were far from pleased. They told Pilate, "Do not write, 'The King of the Jews' but 'This man said, I am King of the Jews.'" Pilate refused: "What I have written I have written." Think about the significance of this inscription. Why were the Jews upset by it? What might have been Pilate's motive for writing it and refusing to change it?

9. As He was being crucified, Jesus said, "Father, forgive them; for they do not know what they are doing." Ponder these words.

10. Jesus was crucified between two criminals. The Greek word Matthew and Mark use to describe the two indicates that they were violent thieves who used force to rob people. Luke uses an even stronger word that suggests that they were workers or authors of evil.[39] Think about the significance of Jesus being crucified between these two men.

11. Matthew and Mark portray the two criminals as taunting Jesus. Luke further describes how one of them had a sudden change of heart. As his fellow thief derided Jesus and said, "Are You not the Messiah? Save Yourself and us," the converting robber admitted that he was getting exactly what his deeds deserved. He testified that Jesus had done nothing wrong, and he humbly requested,

Rosary Meditations

"Jesus, remember me when You come into Your Kingdom." Jesus must have looked at him with love when He replied, "Truly I tell you, today you will be with Me in Paradise." Picture this scene of repentance and forgiveness. What brought about the thief's change of heart? What did he mean when he spoke of Jesus' Kingdom? How did the thief feel when he heard Jesus' words of comfort and promise?

12. The crowd mocked Jesus as He hung on the cross, taunting Him and telling Him to save Himself and come down that they might believe in Him. Why did the crowd do this? What message does this incident send about the nature of faith?

13. Several faithful women, including Jesus' mother, stood near the cross. Imagine what they might have been thinking and feeling.

14. Jesus' beloved disciple, St. John, was standing with Mary. When Jesus saw them, He said to His mother, "Woman, behold your son." Then He said to the disciple, "Behold your mother." With these words, Jesus gave Mary as a mother to the whole human race, which was represented by St. John. Ponder this beautiful truth.

15. As He approached His death, Jesus called out, "Eli, Eli lema sacbachthani," which means "My God, My God, why have You forsaken Me?" Meditate on Jesus' sense of abandonment.

16. Jesus then said, "I am thirsty." Was His thirst merely physical or something more?

The Crucifixion

17. Someone soaked a sponge in sour wine and held it up for Jesus to drink. Examine Dr. Scott Hahn's article about the Fourth Cup and ponder the significance of this action.[40]

18. Darkness covered the whole land until three o'clock in the afternoon when Jesus died. Why?

19. Jesus cried out in a loud voice, "It is finished!" and breathed His last. Reflect on Jesus' final words. Meditate on the death of the God-Man.

20. When Jesus died, the curtain in the Temple was torn in two from top to bottom. This was the curtain that separated the Holy of Holies, God's dwelling place, from the rest of the Temple and, indeed, from the world. What is the meaning of the torn curtain?

21. The earth shook at the moment of Jesus' death. Rocks split. Tombs opened. Ponder these events.

22. One of the Roman soldiers pierced Jesus' side with a lance as He hung dead on the cross, and blood and water poured out. Many saints have taught that the blood and water symbolize the sacraments of the Eucharist and baptism. They have also explained that, at this moment, the Church was born from Jesus' side, just as Eve was born from Adam's side. Reflect on these ideas.

23. The same soldier loudly proclaimed Jesus' innocence, even announcing that He must have been the Son of God. Why did this man experience such a complete change of heart so quickly?

Rosary Meditations

24. Pilate released Jesus' body to Joseph of Arimathea. Joseph wrapped the body and laid it in his own new tomb that had been hewn from the rock. Nicodemus brought a hundred pounds of myrrh and aloes to perform the Jewish burial customs, which had to be abbreviated because of the approaching sabbath. Joseph and Nicodemus rolled a large stone in front of the tomb's opening and went away until after the sabbath. Meditate on the loving care with which Jesus' disciples performed His burial.

25. Mary Magdalene and at least one other woman remained sitting opposite the tomb. Why? Ponder their lonely vigil.

Application Questions

1. What do you feel when You think about Jesus being nailed to the cross and then hanging there, left to die?

2. Do you understand that Jesus suffered and died for you? How might your life be different if you reflected on this truth more often?

3. How do you handle your pain? Do you unite it with Jesus' sufferings? Why or why not?

4. Is Jesus the king of your life? How so? How might you allow Him to reign over you even more?

5. Are you able to forgive those who hurt you? Why or why not?

The Crucifixion

6. When have you experienced the humble repentance that the thief expressed on the cross? How did Jesus responded to you?

7. Is your faith strong? Why or why not? Do you expect God to provide signs in order for you to believe?

8. What is your relationship with Mary? Is she your mother?

9. Have you ever felt abandoned by God? What were the circumstances? How did you respond?

10. Have you ever lost someone you loved? How did that feel? How did you cope with it? Did you turn to Jesus for help? Why or why not?

<u>Prayer, Prayer, and More Prayer</u>

Blessing and Adoration – Dearest Jesus, we bow our heads in silent adoration as we contemplate You on the cross. We fall before You as we meditate on Your suffering and death. We offer our lives to You, Who gave Your life for us.

Praise – Jesus, we praise You as we contemplate You on the cross. We praise You for Your great, self-sacrificing love. We praise You for Your courage, Your humility, and Your strength. We praise You for Your willingness to suffer to save us, for Your commitment to doing Your Father's will no matter what the cost. We praise You for the cross, dearest Jesus.

Thanksgiving – Jesus, thank You. It seems too little to merely say it, especially after Your great suffering and death on the cross. Please help us to live our thanks, to express it in our lives by loving You and our neighbors.

Intercession – Jesus, we lift up to You all those who are suffering. Hold them close to You and comfort them. We lift up to You those who are watching their loved ones suffer. Give them strength, courage, and compassion. We lift up sinners. Give them a repentant heart. We lift up those who behave in a cruel, taunting way. Change their hearts. We lift up those who are grieving. Wrap them up in Your loving arms.

Petition – Jesus, please give us strength in suffering, compassion for those in pain, repentance for our sins, and comfort in our grief. We join the repentant thief in praying, "Jesus, remember me when You come into Your Kingdom."

Quotes from the Saints

"Such is the place of the cross, set up in the center of the earth, that it might be equally free to all nations to attain the knowledge of God." - St. Hilary

"This which was now done to Christ had been prophesied in the Psalm, *They parted my garments among them, and cast lots upon my vesture.* It proceeds, *And sitting down, they watched Him there.* This watchfulness of the soldiers and of the Priests has proved of use to us in making the power of His Resurrection greater and more notorious. *And they set up over His head His accusation written, This is Jesus, the King of the Jews.* I cannot sufficiently wonder at the enormity of the thing, that having purchased false witnesses, and having stirred up the unhappy people to riot and uproar, they found no

The Crucifixion

other plea for putting Him to death, than that He was King of the Jews; and this perhaps they set up in mockery." - St. Jerome

"Two thieves were crucified with him, one on the right hand and one on the left, that in the figure of His cross might be represented that separation of all mankind which shall be made in His judgment. The Passion then of Christ contains a sacrament of our salvation, and of that instrument which the wickedness of the Jews provided for His punishment, the power of the Redeemer made a step to glory." - St. Leo

"Because the Lord had said, *Pray for them that persecute you*, this likewise He did, when He ascended the cross, as it follows, *Then said Jesus, Father, forgive them*, not that He was not able Himself to pardon them, but that He might teach us to pray for our persecutors, not only in word, but in deed also. But He says, *Forgive them*, if they should repent. For He is gracious to the penitent, if they are willing after so great wickedness to wash away their guilt by faith." - St. John Chrysostom

"Now our Lord being truly the Savior wished not by saving Himself, but by saving His creatures, to be acknowledged the Savior. For neither is a physician by healing himself known to be physician, unless he also gives proof of his skill towards the sick. So the Lord being the Savior had no need of salvation, nor by descending from the cross did He wish to be acknowledged the Savior, but by dying. For truly a much greater salvation does the death of the Savior bring to men, than the descent from the cross." - St. Anthanasius

Rosary Meditations

"A most remarkable example is here given of seeking after conversion, seeing that pardon is so speedily granted to the thief. The Lord quickly pardons, because the thief is quickly converted. And grace is more abundant than prayer; for the Lord ever gives more than He is asked for. The thief asked that He should remember him, but our Lord answers, *Verily I say to you, This day shall you be with Me in Paradise.* To be with Christ is life, and where Christ is, there is His Kingdom." - St. Ambrose

"Mary the mother of our Lord stood before the cross of her Son. None of the Evangelists hath told me this except John. The others have related how that at our Lord's Passion the earth quaked, the heaven was overspread with darkness, the sun fled, the thief was taken into paradise after confession. John hath told us, what the others have not, how that from the cross whereon He hung, He called to His mother. He thought it a greater thing to show Him victorious over punishment, fulfilling the offices of piety to His mother, than giving the Kingdom of Heaven and eternal life to the thief. For if it was religious to give life to the thief, a much richer work of piety it is for a Son to honor His mother with such affection. *Behold*, He says, *your son; behold your mother.* Christ made His Testament from the cross, and divided the offices of piety between the Mother and the disciples. Our Lord made not only a public, but also a domestic Testament. And this His Testament John sealed a witness worthy of such a Testator. A good testament it was, not of money, but of eternal life, which was not written with ink, but with the spirit of the living God: *My tongue is the pen of a ready writer*. Mary, as became the mother of our Lord, stood before the cross, when the Apostles fled and with pitiful eyes beheld the wounds of

The Crucifixion

her Son. For she looked not on the death of the Hostage, but on the salvation of the world; and perhaps knowing that her Son's death would bring this salvation, she who had been the habitation of the King, thought that by her death she might add to that universal gift." - St. Ambrose

"When now nought of suffering remains to be endured, death still lingers, knowing that it has nothing there. The ancient foe suspected somewhat unusual. This Man, first and only, he found having no sin, free from guilt, owing nothing to the laws of his jurisdiction. But leagued with Jewish madness, Death comes again to the assault, and desperately invades the Life-giver. And Jesus, when He had cried again with a loud voice, yielded up the ghost. Wherefore should we be offended that Christ came from the bosom of the Father to take upon Him our bondage, that He might confer on us His freedom; to take upon Him our death, that we might be set free by His death; by despising death He exalted us mortals into gods, counted them of earth worthy of things in Heaven? For seeing the Divine power shines forth so brilliant in the contemplation of its works, it is an argument of boundless love, that it suffers for its subjects, dies for its bondsmen. This then was the first cause of the Lord's Passion, that He would have it known how great God's love to man, Who desired rather to be loved than feared. The second was that He might abolish with yet more justice the sentence of death which He had with justice passed. For as the first man had by guilt incurred death through God's sentence, and handed down the same to his posterity, the second Man, who knew no sin, came from heaven that death might be condemned, which, when commissioned to seize the guilty, had presumed to touch the Author of sinlessness. And it is no wonder if for us He laid down what He had taken of us, His life,

Rosary Meditations

namely, when He has done other so great things for us, and bestowed so much on us." - St. Augustine

"Nor without meaning has one Evangelist spoken of a new tomb, another of the tomb of Joseph. For the grave is prepared by those who are under the law of death; the Conqueror of death has no grave of His own. For what fellowship has God with the grave. He alone is enclosed in this tomb, because the death of Christ, although it was common according to the nature of the body, yet was it peculiar in respect of power. But Christ is rightly buried in the tomb of the just, that He may rest in the habitation of justice. For this monument the just man hews out with the piercing word in the hearts of Gentile hardness, that the power of Christ might extend over the nations. And very rightly is there a stone rolled against the tomb; for whoever has in himself truly buried Christ, must diligently guard, lest he lose Him, or lest there be an entrance for unbelief." - St. Ambrose

The First Glorious Mystery: The Resurrection

Scripture References

Matthew 27:62-28:20; Mark 16:1-20; Luke 24:1-53; John 20:1-21:24

The Story in Brief

Jesus is risen! On the third day after His crucifixion, He rose from the dead. An angel rolled away the stone blocking the tomb's entrance and announced to Jesus' female disciples that their Lord had risen. Jesus Himself then appeared to Mary Magdalene, to several other women, to two disciples on the road to Emmaus, and to a group of disciples who were hiding from the Jews. Eight days later, He appeared again, this time relieving the doubt of the apostle Thomas, who had declined to believe until he placed his fingers in the wounds on Jesus' hands and his hand in the wound in His side. Jesus also appeared to His disciples while they were fishing in Galilee. At His command, they lowered their nets and miraculously caught 153 large fish. After preparing breakfast on the shore, Jesus asked Peter three times, "Simon, son of John, do you love Me?" When Peter replied to the affirmative, Jesus ordered Him to care for His sheep. Before Jesus ascended into Heaven, He commissioned the disciples to spread the Gospel and to

Rosary Meditations

baptize all nations in the Name of the Father, of the Son, and of the Holy Spirit. He promised to be with them always.

Points to Ponder

1. Take a few minutes to ponder the silence of Jesus' tomb.

2. The Creed tells us that Jesus descended into hell (i.e., into the realm of the dead). Saints and mystics teach us that Jesus spoke with the patriarchs and matriarchs of the Old Testament and prepared them to go with Him to Heaven, for by His death, He had opened Heaven's gates.[41] Picture the scene, and imagine the conversations between Jesus and the faithful men and women of the Old Testament.

3. Matthew says that the Jews asked Pilate to place a guard of soldiers by Jesus' tomb, for they were afraid that someone might steal Jesus' body. Pilate did as they requested and told them to make the tomb as secure as possible. The Jews set the guard and sealed the stone at the tomb's entrance. How did the Jews' paranoia strengthen the evidence in favor of Jesus' Resurrection?

4. Jesus rose on the first day of the week, which is the day after the Jewish sabbath and our Sunday. Theologians have pointed out that the first day of the week symbolizes a new creation.[42] God created the world in six days and rested on the seventh, the sabbath. Now, on the eighth day, Jesus has recreated the world. Reflect on these ideas.

5. Early in the morning, several of Jesus' female disciples went to the tomb. They knew that a heavy stone blocked

The Resurrection

the entrance, and they may even have been aware of the guard. The women realized that they would have a difficult time getting into the tomb, but they set out anyway. Meditate on their faithfulness and courage.

6. In Matthew's account, an angel descended from heaven with a great earthquake. The angel rolled away the stone and sat just above it. He was dressed in white and glowed like lightning. Seeing him, the guards started shaking and then fainted. Why did the angel appear in such a dramatic fashion?

7. As the women approached the angel, the first words he spoke were "Do not be afraid." These words appear 365 times in the Bible, one for each day of the year. Why do we need to hear them so often?

8. The angel continued, "I know that you are looking for Jesus Who was crucified. He is not here; for He has been raised, as He said. Come, see the place where He lay." By the time the angel spoke with the women, Jesus was no longer in the tomb. Think about that. Jesus rose from the dead. Death could not hold Him. He rose up victorious.

9. Mark's account also relates the women's encounter with the angel, whom the evangelist describes as a young man dressed in a white robe. The angel was sitting in the tomb on the right side. What is the significance of the right side?

10. St. Luke speaks of two men in dazzling clothes who met the women at the tomb. Why does Luke mention two angels? The women were terrified, but the angels asked them, "Why do you look for the living among the dead?

Rosary Meditations

He is not here, but has risen." Meditate on the living Jesus, risen from the dead.

11. St. John informs us that when Mary Magdalene saw that the tomb was empty, she immediately ran to get Peter and John. Ponder Mary's urgency.

12. The angel sent the women back to the disciples to announce the Resurrection and tell them that Jesus was going ahead of them to Galilee. Reflect on how these women became evangelists to the disciples.

13. At least some of the disciples refused to believe the women's words, which seemed like an "idle tale." Consider the disciples' hesitancy to believe. What were they thinking and feeling?

14. Peter and John, however, paid enough attention to Mary Magdalene to realize that Jesus' tomb was empty. In fact, according to John's account, Mary seems to have left the tomb before hearing the angel's message, for when she spoke to the disciples, she was rather panicky and announced, "They have taken the Lord out of the tomb, and we do not know where they have laid Him." Reflect on Mary's words and state of mind. What did she feel when she saw the empty tomb?

15. Peter and John hurried to the tomb. They saw the burial cloths lying empty and the cloth that had been on Jesus' head rolled up in a corner by itself. Even though they did not yet understand, they began to believe. Think about the relationship between faith and understanding.

16. Mary Magdalene stood weeping outside the tomb. Angels appeared and asked her why she was crying.

The Resurrection

"They have taken away my Lord, and I do not know where they have laid Him," she replied. Ponder Mary's heartbreak.

17. Then Mary saw Jesus, but she did not know Who He was. Why not?

18. Mary begged the Man she thought was a gardener to tell her where He had laid her Lord that she might go and take Him away. Jesus said one word to her: "Mary." Visualize this exchange.

19. Then Mary knew. She turned and cried out "Rabbouni!" How and why did Mary recognize Jesus?

20. Jesus told Mary not to cling to Him because He had not yet ascended to the Father. Why did Jesus not want Mary to cling to Him?

21. Meditate on the relationship between the risen Jesus and His followers. How was their interaction the same as before? How was it different?

22. Ponder Mary's joy in the resurrected Jesus.

23. According to Matthew's Gospel, the other women also had an encounter with Jesus. They fell down before Him and worshiped Him. He told them not to be afraid and to tell His brothers to go to Galilee. These women knew that Jesus had been dead. Now He was standing before them. Reflect on what they were thinking and feeling.

24. Read the story of the disciples on the road to Emmaus in Luke 24:13-35. Why were they leaving Jerusalem and heading to Emmaus? What were they thinking and

Rosary Meditations

feeling? Why did they not recognize Jesus? What kinds of things did Jesus tell them when He interpreted the Scriptures for them? Why did they recognize Jesus when He took bread and blessed it? What was the significance of this action? Ponder how the disciples' hearts burned within them when Jesus spoke to them. Why did the disciples return to Jerusalem immediately?

25. Jesus appeared to His disciples before they went to Galilee. Why did He choose to make Himself known to them earlier than He had indicated?

26. The disciples were hiding out. They had locked the door because they feared the Jews. Why were they afraid?

27. Jesus came to His disciples through the locked door. How did they feel when they saw the risen Jesus? What did He look like? What proofs did He give them of His Resurrection? Ponder Jesus' resurrected Body and the disciples' response to Him.

28. Jesus greeted the disciples, saying "Peace be with you." What is the peace that Jesus brings?

29. Meditate on doubting Thomas and his proclamation of faith. Think about Thomas' doubt, his demand for physical proof, Jesus' patience with him, and Jesus' promise that those who have not seen and have believed will be blessed.

30. Reflect on the miracle in Galilee. Why had the disciples decided to go fishing? Why did they not recognize Jesus at first? What was the meaning of their miraculous catch? Why did Peter jump into the water and start swimming for shore? What was the significance of

The Resurrection

the breakfast Jesus prepared? How did the disciples come to understand that Jesus was with them?

31. Jesus asked Peter three times, "Do you love Me?" Ponder this conversation. Why did Jesus ask three times? What does it mean to care for Jesus' sheep?

32. Jesus commissioned the disciples: "Go therefore and make disciples of all the nations, baptizing them in the name of the Father and of the Son, and of the Holy Spirit, and teaching them to obey everything that I have commanded you. And remember, I am with You always, to the end of the age." Ponder Jesus' words and the disciples' mission.

33. Each of the Gospels presents a slightly different description of the Resurrection events. Why is that? How might the variances among the accounts actually increase the evangelists' credibility as well as the sense of mystery surrounding the Resurrection?

34. Several websites, including New Advent and Tekton Education and Apologetics, offer interesting harmonizations of the Gospel accounts.[43] After reading one or two of these harmonizations, think about whether or not they increase your understanding of the Resurrection event.

Application Questions

1. Have you ever experienced a situation in which there was nothing you could do for someone you love? How did that make you feel?

2. What makes you afraid? How do you conquer your fears?

3. What does Jesus' victory over death mean to you? How does it affect your life?

4. Has God ever done anything dramatic in your life? What?

5. Do you ever look for the living among the dead? Is your attention focused on things that will not bring you true life and happiness? What kinds of things? How might you change that focus?

6. How do you spread the Word of God as an evangelist to the world around you?

7. Are you ever hesitant to believe in God or in the teachings of the Church? In what circumstances? How do you overcome your hesitancy?

8. How do you respond to grief?

9. When have you had trouble recognizing Jesus in your life?

10. Do you ever cling to the ways of the past instead of moving forward into the present and toward the future? How might you let go and surrender yourself to God?

11. Are you joyful in your faith? Why or why not? How might you increase your joy?

The Resurrection

12. Have you ever felt your heart burn within you as you read the Scriptures or received the sacraments? What was the experience like?

13. Do you spend time reading and meditating on the Scriptures daily? Why or why not?

14. How do you experience the peace of Jesus?

15. Have you ever been a "doubting Thomas"? Why or why not? If you have been, what changed your heart and mind?

16. How are you called to care for Jesus' sheep?

17. What kind of relationship do you have with the risen Jesus?

18. Do you remember that Jesus is with you always? How would such a recollection change your life?

Prayer, Prayer, and More Prayer

Blessing and Adoration – Risen Jesus, we bow before You in silent adoration as we contemplate Your victory over death in and through Your Resurrection. We join with the disciples in wonder and awe as we greet You, the One Who once was dead but now is alive.

Praise – Jesus, we praise You for Your glorious Resurrection. We praise You for the empty tomb. We praise You for the message of the angels. We praise you for Your appearances to Your disciples. We praise You for that wonderful walk to Emmaus. We praise You for the miraculous catch and the breakfast by the shore. We praise You for being You, our risen Lord.

Thanksgiving – Jesus, we thank You for Your Resurrection and for Your victory over death, a victory that becomes our victory, too, when we surrender ourselves to You in faith, hope, and love.

Intercession – Jesus, we lift up to You all those who doubt. Touch their hearts, Lord, and soften them to accept the faith You are so ready to give. We lift up those who grieve. Comfort them, Lord. We lift up all bishops, priests, and deacons, for they have a special responsibility to care for Your sheep. Give them strength, courage, faithfulness, and especially, love.

Petition – Jesus, strengthen our faith. Help us to encounter You, our risen Lord, and to see You in our neighbors and in the events of our lives. May we always recognize You, especially in the breaking of the bread, and may the words of the Scared Scriptures always make our hearts burn within us.

Quotes from the Saints

"He rose again after three days, to signify the consent of the whole Trinity in the passion of the Son; the three days' space is read figuratively, because the Trinity which in the beginning made man, the same in the end restores man by the passion of Christ." - St. Augustine

"*And, behold, there was a great earthquake.* Our Lord, Son at once of God and man, according to His twofold nature of Godhead and of flesh, gives a sign one while of His greatness, another while of His lowliness. Thus,

The Resurrection

though now it was man who was crucified, and man who was buried, yet the things that were done around show the Son of God." - St. Jerome

"He said not 'rolled,' but rolled back; because the rolling to of the stone was a proof of death; the rolling it back asserted the Resurrection. The order of things is changed; The Tomb devours death, and not the dead; the house of death becomes the mansion of life; a new law is imposed upon it, it receives a dead, and renders up a living, man. It follows, *And sat thereon.* He sat down, who was incapable of weariness; but sat as a teacher of the faith, a master of the Resurrection; upon the stone, that the firmness of his seat might assure the steadfastness of the believers; the Angel rested the foundations of the Faith upon that rock, on which Christ was to found His Church. Or, by the stone of the sepulcher may be denoted death, under which we all lay; and by the Angel sitting thereon, is shown that Christ has by His might subdued death." - St. Peter Chrysologus

"According to the mystical meaning, by the women coming early in the morning to the sepulcher, we have an example given us, that having cast away the darkness of our vices, we should come to the Body of the Lord. For that sepulcher also bore the figure of the Altar of the Lord, wherein herein the mysteries of Christ's Body, not in silk or purple cloth, but in pure white linen, like that in which Joseph wrapped it, ought to be consecrated, that as He offered up to death for us the true substance of His earthly nature, so we also in commemoration of Him should place on the Altar the flax, pure from the plant of the earth, and white, and in many ways refined by a kind of crushing to death. But the spices which the women bring, signify the odor of virtue, and the sweetness of

Rosary Meditations

prayers by which we ought to approach the Altar. The rolling back of the stone alludes to the unclosing of the Sacraments which were concealed by the veil of the letter of the law which was written on stone, the covering of which being taken away, the dead body of the Lord is not found, but the living body is preached; for although we have known Christ according to the flesh, yet now henceforth know we Him no more. But as when the Body of our Lord lay in the sepulcher, Angels are said to have stood by, so also at the time of consecration are they to be believed to stand by the mysteries of Christ. Let us then after the example of the devout women, whenever we approach the heavenly mysteries because of the presence of the Angels, or from reverence to the Sacred Offering, with all humility, bow our faces to the earth, recollecting that we are but dust and ashes." - St. Bede

"A twofold feeling possessed the minds of the women, fear and joy; fear, at the greatness of the miracle; joy, in their desire of Him that was risen; but both added speed to their women's steps, as it follows, *And did run to bring His disciples word*. They went to the Apostles, that through them might be spread abroad the seed of the faith. They who thus desired, and who thus ran, merited to have their rising Lord come to meet them; whence it follows, *And, behold, Jesus met them, saying, All hail.*" - St. Jerome

"[Mary Magdalene] sought the body, and found it not; she persevered in seeking; and so it came to pass that she found. Her longings growing the stronger, the more they were disappointed, at last found and laid hold on their object. For holy longings ever gain strength by delay, did they not, they would not be longings. Mary so loved, that not content with seeing the sepulcher, she stooped down

The Resurrection

and looked in: let us see the fruit which came of this persevering love: *And sees two Angels in white sitting, the one at the head, and the other at the feet, where the body of Jesus had lain...*" - St. Gregory the Great

"Consider the mercy of the Lord, how for the sake of one soul, He exhibits His wounds. And yet the disciples deserved credit, and He had Himself foretold the event. Notwithstanding, because one person, Thomas, would examine Him, Christ allowed him. But He did not appear to him immediately, but waited till the eighth day, in order that the admonition being given in the presence of the disciples, might kindle in him greater desire, and strengthen his faith for the future. And after eight days again His disciples were within, and Thomas with them: then came Jesus, the doors being shut, and stood in the midst, and said, *Peace be to you*....And first He rebukes him; then says He to Thomas, *Reach hither your finger, and behold My hands; and reach hither your hand, and thrust it into My side*: secondly, He admonishes him; *And be not faithless, but believing*. Note how that before they receive the Holy Ghost faith wavers, but afterward is firm. We may wonder how an incorruptible body could retain the marks of the nails. But it was done in condescension; in order that they might be sure that it was the very Person Who was crucified." - St. John Chrysostom

"Let us then reverence the gift of peace, which Christ when He departed hence left to us. Peace both in name and reality is sweet, which also we have heard to be of God, as it is said, *The peace of God*; and that God is of it, as He is our peace. Peace is a blessing commended by all, but observed by few. What then is the cause? Perhaps the desire of dominion or riches, or the envy or hatred of our neighbor, or some one of those vices into which we see men fall who know not God. For peace is peculiarly of God, Who binds all things together in one, to Whom nothing so much belongs as the unity of nature, and a peaceful condition. It is borrowed indeed by angels and divine powers, which are peacefully disposed towards God and one another. It is diffused through the whole creation, whose glory is tranquility. But in us it abides in our souls indeed by the following and imparting of the virtues, in our bodies by the harmony of our members and organs, of which the one is called beauty, the other health." - St. Gregory of Nazianzus

"And because what He had laid upon them was great, therefore to exalt their spirits He adds, *And, lo, I am with you always, even to the end of the world.* As much as to say, Tell Me not of the difficulty of these things, seeing I am with you, Who can make all things easy. A like promise He often made to the Prophets in the Old Testament, to Jeremiah who pleaded his youth, to Moses, and to Ezekiel, when they would have shunned the office imposed upon them. And not with them only does He say that He will be, but with all who shall believe after them. For the Apostles were not to continue till the end of the world, but He says this to the faithful as to one body." - St. John Chrysostom

The Second Glorious Mystery: The Ascension

Scripture References

Luke 24:50-53; Acts 1:6-11

The Story in Brief

Jesus appeared to His disciples for forty days after His Resurrection. On the day of His Ascension, the disciples gathered together and asked Jesus if the time had come for Him to restore the Kingdom to Israel. He replied that it was not their place to know the times set by the Father, but they would receive the power of the Holy Spirit and be His witnesses to the ends of the earth. When He finished speaking and blessing His disciples, He was lifted up before their eyes, and a cloud took Him from their sight. While they were still gazing intently at the sky, two men in white robes appeared and asked them why they were standing there looking up toward Heaven. These mysterious men promised the disciples that Jesus would return the same way as they saw Him ascend.

Points to Ponder

1. Jesus appeared to the disciples over the course of forty days and spoke with them about the Kingdom of God.

Rosary Meditations

Why did Jesus appear for forty days? What is the Kingdom of God?

2. At the end of the forty days, the disciples gathered together with Jesus. Think about how much the disciples already valued the practice of assembling as a community.

3. The disciples asked Jesus, "Lord, is this the time when You will restore the Kingdom to Israel?" What kind of kingdom did they envision? Was their idea of a kingdom different from that of Jesus?

4. Reflect on Jesus' response to His disciples: "It is not for you to know the times or periods that the Father has set by His own authority." Reflect on the significance of mystery.

5. Jesus promised the disciples that they would receive power when the Holy Spirit came upon them and that they would be witnesses to Him throughout Jerusalem, Judea, and Samaria and to the ends of the earth. Ponder the power of the Holy Spirit.

6. Reflect on how Christianity has spread to the ends of the earth.

7. What does it mean to witness to Jesus?

8. According to Luke's Gospel, Jesus raised His hands and blessed His disciples before He ascended. Reflect on the meaning of this gesture.

The Ascension

9. After He had spoken, Jesus was lifted up before His disciples' eyes, and a cloud took Him from their sight. Envision the scene. What is the meaning of the cloud?

10. Why did Jesus ascend to Heaven in a visible way? He might simply have disappeared. Recall that even in His risen state, Jesus is still fully God and fully Man. Remember also that He accommodates Himself to His disciples' needs.

11. Jesus both ascended to Heaven by His own power and was lifted up by His Father. Why is this not a contradiction?

12. After Jesus ascended, the disciples stood in awe, gazing up toward Heaven. Imagine their expressions. Note that the Greek word translated here as "gazing" suggests looking steadfastly and even stretching or straining one's eyes in order to see.[44]

13. Suddenly, two men in white robes appeared beside them and asked, "Men of Galilee, why do you stand looking up toward Heaven?" Think about the implications of this question. Why did the two men ask it? How did the disciples have to redirect their gaze now that Jesus had ascended into Heaven?

14. The two men continued, "This Jesus, Who has been taken up from you into Heaven, will come in the same way you saw Him go into Heaven." Ponder these words, which offered the disciples both reassurance and a promise.

15. Who were the two men in white robes?

Rosary Meditations

16. In the Creed, we say that Jesus "ascended into Heaven and is seated at the right hand of the Father." What does it mean for Jesus to sit at the Father's right hand?

17. Jesus ascended into Heaven as the God-Man with a glorified human body. Ponder this awesome truth.

18. Imagine the welcome Jesus received in Heaven.

Application Questions

1. How do you understand the Kingdom of God? In what ways are you already living in the Kingdom?

2. How important is it to you to assemble with other Christians?

3. Are you able to accept mystery? Why or why not?

4. How is the Holy Spirit working in your life? Do you have a relationship with the Holy Spirit?

5. How do you witness to Jesus? How might you extend your witness?

6. How would you have responded to the Ascension if you had been standing in the disciples' place?

7. Have you ever stood in awe of something God did in your life or someone else's life? What was that experience like?

8. Have you ever been in a situation in which you had to redirect your gaze? What were the circumstances?

The Ascension

9. Is Jesus Christ the King of your life? If so, how has His reign changed you?

10. Do you look forward to the time when you will be in Heaven with Jesus? What images of Heaven do you treasure?

<u>Prayer, Prayer, and More Prayer</u>

Blessing and Adoration – Dearest Jesus, we bow before You in silent adoration as we contemplate You seated at the right hand of the Father. We fall before You in wonder and awe, knowing that although You are fully human like us, You are also fully divine, and You reign with Your Father and the Holy Spirit in Heaven.

Praise – Jesus, we praise You for Your Ascension. We praise You for being completely awe-inspiring. We praise You for Your glorious reign as king of the universe.

Thanksgiving – Thank You, Jesus, for always keeping Your promises. At Your Ascension, You promised to send the Holy Spirit down upon Your disciples, and You did. You still send Him down upon us today. Thank You, Jesus, for the gift of the Holy Spirit.

Intercession – Lord, we lift up to You the missionaries who work to spread Christianity to the ends of the earth. Guard them and guide them, Lord. We lift up those who are outside the Church and do not understand the importance of gathering with other Christians. Touch their hearts, Lord, and bring them home to Your Church.

Petition – Lord, please give us the strength and courage we need to be Your witnesses to the ends of the earth.

Rosary Meditations

Please enkindle within us a strong appreciation for mystery. Help us to realize that we need not understand everything in order to have great faith.

Quotes from the Saints

"Christ is already in that place of peace, which is all in all. He is on the right hand of God. He is hidden in the brightness of the radiance which issues from the everlasting throne. He is in the very abyss of peace, where there is no voice of tumult or distress, but a deep stillness--stillness, that greatest and most awful of all goods which we can fancy; that most perfect of joys, the utter profound, ineffable tranquility of the Divine Essence. He has entered into His rest. That is our home; here we are on a pilgrimage, and Christ calls us to His many mansions which He has prepared." - Blessed John Henry Newman[45]

"Today our Lord Jesus Christ ascended into heaven; let our hearts ascend with him. Listen to the words of the Apostle: *If you have risen with Christ, set your hearts on the things that are above where Christ is, seated at the right hand of God; seek the things that are above, not the things that are on earth.* For just as He remained with us even after His Ascension, so we too are already in Heaven with Him, even though what is promised us has not yet been fulfilled in our bodies." - St. Augustine

"I answer that Christ's Ascension is the cause of our salvation in two ways: first of all, on our part; secondly, on His. On our part, in so far as by the Ascension our souls are uplifted to Him; because...His Ascension fosters, first, faith; secondly, hope; thirdly, charity. Fourthly, our reverence for Him is thereby increased,

The Ascension

since we no longer deem Him an earthly man, but the God of Heaven; thus the Apostle says (2 Corinthians 5:16): *If we have known Christ according to the flesh — that is, as mortal, whereby we reputed Him as a mere man*, as the gloss interprets the words — *but now we know Him so no longer.* On His part, in regard to those things which, in ascending, He did for our salvation. First, He prepared the way for our ascent into Heaven, according to His own saying (John 14:2): *I go to prepare a place for you*, and the words of Micheas (2:13), *He shall go up that shall open the way before them.* For since He is our Head the members must follow whither the Head has gone: hence He said (John 14:3): *That where I am, you also may be.* In sign whereof He took to Heaven the souls of the saints delivered from hell, according to Psalm 67:19 (Cf. Ephesians 4:8): *Ascending on high, He led captivity captive*, because He took with Him to Heaven those who had been held captives by the devil — to Heaven, as to a place strange to human nature; captives in deed of a happy taking, since they were acquired by His victory. Secondly, because as the high-priest under the Old Testament entered the holy place to stand before God for the people, so also Christ entered Heaven *to make intercession for us*, as is said in Hebrews 7:25. Because the very showing of Himself in the human nature which He took with Him to Heaven is a pleading for us, so that for the very reason that God so exalted human nature in Christ, He may take pity on them for whom the Son of God took human nature. Thirdly, that being established in His heavenly seat as God and Lord, He might send down gifts upon men, according to Ephesians 4:10: *He ascended above all the heavens, that He might fill all things, that is, with His gifts*, according to the gloss." - St. Thomas Aquinas[46]

Rosary Meditations

"But you will say, How does this concern me? Because you also shall be taken up in like manner into the clouds. For your body is of like nature to His body, therefore shall your body be so light, that it can pass through the air. For as is the head, so also is the body; as the beginning, so also the end. See then how you are honored by this beginning. Man was the lowest part of the rational creation, but the feet have been made the head, being lifted up aloft into the royal throne in their Head." - St. John Chrysostom

The Third Glorious Mystery: The Descent of the Holy Spirit

Scripture References

Acts 2:1-42; John 14:15-31

The Story in Brief

For nine days after Jesus' Ascension into Heaven, the disciples gathered together to pray for the coming of the Holy Spirit. On the day of Pentecost, they were together in one place. A noise like a strong, driving wind filled the house, and tongues as of fire rested on each of them. They were filled with the Holy Spirit and began to speak in different tongues as the Spirit inspired them. Jews from all over the world were gathered in Jerusalem for Pentecost. Hearing the commotion, they flocked to the house where the disciples were. The crowd was amazed, for each person heard the disciples speaking in his own language about the great deeds of God. Peter then stood up and preached a sermon, explaining to the crowd how Jesus, the Messiah, had fulfilled the prophecies contained in Scripture and how He had suffered, died, and rose again and was now pouring out the Holy Spirit. He invited the Jews to repent and be baptized so that their sins might be forgiven and they, too, might receive the gift of the Spirit. Three thousand people were baptized that day, and with the rest of the Christian community, they devoted themselves to the apostles' teaching, fellowship, the breaking of the bread, and prayers.

Points to Ponder

1. The descent of the Holy Spirit took place on the Jewish feast of Pentecost. For the Jews, Pentecost occurred fifty days after the first post-Passover sabbath. It was commonly known as the "feast of weeks" or the "feast of harvest of the first fruits," and it commemorated both the harvest and the end of the Paschal season. At Pentecost, the Jews remembered how God gave the Law to Moses on Mount Sinai fifty days after the Israelites fled Egypt.[47] Reflect on how the Christian Pentecost both fulfills and elevates the Jewish Pentecost.

2. On Pentecost, the disciples were all together in one place, praying. Why does Luke mention this specifically? What is the significance of the disciples' common prayer?

3. Many saints and scholars have remarked that the nine days between Jesus' Ascension and Pentecost constituted the first novena (i.e., nine days of prayer for a particular intention). What was the disciples' special prayer intention?

4. The Holy Spirit arrived with a sound like a violent wind. Meditate on this. Why would the Spirit choose to announce His presence by the sound of wind? Remember that the word "spirit" in Greek is *pneuma*, which derives from the Greek word *pnoē*, meaning "wind."[48]

5. The sound of the wind filled the entire house where the disciples had gathered, so it must have been quite loud. Why did the Spirit manifest Himself so dramatically?

The Descent of the Holy Spirit

6. Luke tells us, "Divided tongues, as of fire, appeared among them, and a tongue rested on each of them." What does fire symbolize? Why is fire a proper symbol for the Holy Spirit? Think especially about fire's purifying, warming, and enlivening qualities.

7. Reflect on how the Holy Spirit touched each disciple personally.

8. The disciples were filled with the Holy Spirit. What does it mean to be filled with the Holy Spirit? What were the disciples experiencing internally?

9. The disciples' encounter with the Holy Spirit did not remain internal. They began to speak out loud in other languages, for the Spirit gave them the ability to do so. What does this miracle signify?

10. Luke informs us that Jews from all over the world were present in Jerusalem for Pentecost. A crowd of these Jews gathered around the house where the disciples were staying. Apparently, something had caught their attention. They were bewildered because each of them heard the disciples speaking in his own language. Picture this scene. How would you have felt if you had been part of the crowd?

11. Many saints and scholars have taught that the miracles of language on Pentecost reversed the consequences of the Tower of Babel. Read the story of the Tower of Babel in Genesis 11, and reflect on this idea.

12. The crowd heard the disciples speaking about God's deeds of power. Meditate on these great deeds. Which ones would the disciples, or rather the Holy Spirit

Rosary Meditations

speaking through the disciples, have emphasized on Pentecost?

13. Some members of the crowd were amazed by what they were seeing and hearing. Others scoffed and said the disciples were "filled with new wine." Reflect especially on the latter group. Why did they refuse to be amazed by what they saw and heard?

14. Think about the accusation that the disciples were "filled with new wine." Did the scoffers touch upon a truth they did not understand? The disciples certainly had not been drinking alcohol, but were they perhaps filled with a very special kind of new wine?

15. Carefully read and ponder Peter's message to the Jews in Acts 2:14-36. Reflect on his proclamation that Jesus had fulfilled the Old Testament prophecies through His life, miracles, death, Resurrection, and Ascension.

16. Peter further announced that Jesus, the crucified Messiah, had been raised up, was seated at God's right hand, and had poured out the Holy Spirit upon the disciples. Read John 14:15-31, and meditate on how Jesus had fulfilled His promises.

17. The Jews were "cut to the heart" by Peter's sermon. What does this mean? Why were the Jews so affected?

18. The Jews asked Peter and the other apostles what they must do. Reflect on their desire to respond to Peter's message.

19. Peter replied, "Repent, and be baptized every one of you in the name of Jesus Christ so that your sins may be

The Descent of the Holy Spirit

forgiven; and you will receive the gift of the Holy Spirit." Ponder the great gifts of repentance, baptism, and forgiveness.

20. Peter continued, assuring the crowd that God's promises were for them, for their children, for those who were far away, and indeed, for everyone called by God. Which promises was he talking about?

21. Peter testified with many other arguments and exhorted the crowd to save themselves from the corrupt generation. The Greek word for "testified" means to solemnly bear witness and to attest to the truth while the Greek word for "exhorted" means to call to one's side.[49] Peter was calling the crowd to join him in following Jesus Christ. Ponder Peter's testimony and exhortation.

22. Three thousand people were baptized that day. Reflect on this great work of the Holy Spirit.

23. The Christian community devoted itself to the apostles' teaching, fellowship, the breaking of the bread (i.e., the Eucharist), and prayers. Meditate on these early Christians and their devotion. How is our modern Christian life similar and different?

24. Ponder the Holy Spirit. Who is He? What is His role in Christian life? Refer to John 14:15-31. Also spend some time examining EWTN's pages about the Holy Spirit.[50]

25. Meditate on the seven gifts of the Holy Spirit: wisdom, knowledge, understanding, counsel, fortitude, piety, and fear of the Lord. Read the article "Gifts of the Holy Spirit" by Fr. William Saunders for more information.[51]

Rosary Meditations

26. Ponder the twelve fruits of the Holy Spirit: charity, joy, peace, patience, kindness, goodness, generosity, gentleness, faithfulness, modesty, self-control, and chastity.

Application Questions

1. How important is it to you to gather and pray with other Christians? What are the advantages of sharing one's faith and prayer with others?

2. How is God trying to get your attention today?

3. What is your current relationship with the Holy Spirit? Does the Third Person of the Blessed Trinity play a major role in your life? Why or why not?

4. Have you ever been filled with the Holy Spirit (think especially about your baptism and confirmation)? What did it feel like? How did you respond?

5. Are you on fire with the Holy Spirit? Why or why not? How might your life be different if you allowed the power of the Spirit to set your heart aflame?

6. Do you need to be purified in your attitudes, thoughts, words, and/or deeds? How so?

7. What deeds of power has God performed in your life? Are you properly amazed by them?

8. Have you ever encountered scoffers who sneer at Christianity? How do you respond to them?

The Descent of the Holy Spirit

9. Do you believe that Jesus always keeps His promises? How has He done so in your life?

10. How are the seven gifts and twelve fruits of the Holy Spirit present and active in your life? In which areas do you need to ask the Holy Spirit to increase His gifts and fruits?

11. Have you ever been "cut to the heart" by something you heard or read? What were the circumstances? How did you feel? How did you respond?

12. How do you testify to Christ and exhort others to join you in following Jesus?

13. How do you devote yourself to the apostles' teaching, fellowship, the Eucharist, and prayers in the Christian community?

<u>Prayer, Prayer, and More Prayer</u>

Blessing and Adoration – Father, Son, and Holy Spirit, Blessed Trinity, Three-in-One, we bow before You in silent adoration as we contemplate the descent of the Holy Spirit at Pentecost. We adore You for Your great power and love that fills the whole world and all of us.

Praise – Holy Spirit, we praise You, for You are our Breath of life. Holy Spirit, we praise You, for You are our Advocate. Holy Spirit, we praise You, for You are our Comforter. Holy Spirit, we praise You, for You are our Guide. Holy Spirit, we praise You. Come to us.

Thanksgiving – Holy Spirit, thank You for filling our hearts with Your power and love. Jesus, thank You for

Rosary Meditations

pouring out Your Holy Spirit upon us. Father, thank You for sending Your Son to be our Savior and the Holy Spirit to be our Advocate.

Intercession – Father, Son, and Holy Spirit, we lift up to You all those who lack faith and those who scoff at Christianity. Touch their hearts and change them. We lift up to You all who are hearing the Christian message for the first time. Open their minds that they may understand and their hearts that they may assent to You. We lift up all those who have abandoned their Catholic faith. Teach them the truth and bring them home.

Petition – Holy Spirit, please pour out upon us Your great gifts of wisdom, knowledge, understanding, counsel, fortitude, piety, and fear of the Lord. Please help us to continually bear Your fruits of charity, joy, peace, patience, kindness, goodness, generosity, gentleness, faithfulness, modesty, self-control, and chastity. Increase all of these in us, Holy Spirit.

Quotes from the Saints

"And there appeared unto them cloven tongues like as of fire, and it sat upon each of them; and they were all filled with the Holy Spirit (Acts 2:3-4). They partook of fire, not of burning but of saving fire; of fire which consumes the thorns of sins, but gives luster to the soul. This is now coming upon you also, and that to strip away and consume your sins which are like thorns, and to brighten yet more that precious possession of your souls, and to give you grace; for He gave it then to the Apostles. And He sat upon them in the form of fiery tongues, that they might crown themselves with new and spiritual diadems by fiery tongues upon their heads. A fiery sword

The Descent of the Holy Spirit

barred of old the gates of Paradise; a fiery tongue which brought salvation restored the gift." - St. Cyril of Jerusalem

"But as the old Confusion of tongues was laudable, when men who were of one language in wickedness and impiety, even as some now venture to be, were building the Tower; for by the confusion of their language the unity of their intention was broken up, and their undertaking destroyed; so much more worthy of praise is the present miraculous one. For being poured from One Spirit upon many men, it brings them again into harmony. And there is a diversity of Gifts, which stands in need of yet another Gift to discern which is the best, where all are praiseworthy." - St. Gregory of Nazianzus

"Was it upon the twelve that [the Holy Spirit] came? Not so; but upon the hundred and twenty. For Peter would not have quoted to no purpose the testimony of the prophet, saying, *And it shall come to pass in the last days, saith the Lord God, I will pour out of My Spirit upon all flesh: and your sons and your daughters shall prophesy, and your young men shall see visions, and your old men shall dream dreams* (Joel 2:28). *And they were all filled with the Holy Spirit.* For, that the effect may not be to frighten only, therefore it is both *with the Holy Spirit, and with fire. And began to speak with other tongues, as the Spirit gave them utterance* (Mt. 3:11)." - St. John Chrysostom

"Jesus tells us that His holy Disciples will be more courageous and more understanding when they would be, as the Scripture says, *Endowed with power from on high* (Luke 24:49), and that when their minds would be illuminated by the torch of the Spirit they would be able

Rosary Meditations

to see into all things, even though no longer able to question Him bodily present among them. The Saviour does not say that they would no longer as before need the light of His guidance, but that when they received His Spirit, when He was dwelling in their hearts, they would not be wanting in any good thing, and their minds would be filled with most perfect knowledge." - St. Cyril of Alexandria

"...For as of old on the fiftieth day after the Sacrifice of the Lamb, the Law was given on Mount Sinai to the Hebrew people, now delivered from the Egyptians, so, after the Passion of Christ, in which the True Lamb of God was slain, on the fiftieth day after His Resurrection, the Holy Spirit descended upon the Apostles and upon the people who believed (Acts 2:3); so that an earnest Christian might know beyond any uncertainty, that the sacred rites of the Old Testament had served as foundations for the Gospel, and that by this same Spirit was the Second Covenant laid down, by Whom the first had been established." - St. Leo the Great

"Through the Holy Spirit comes our restoration to paradise, our ascension into the Kingdom of Heaven, our return to the adoption of sons, our liberty to call God our Father, our being made partakers of the grace of Christ, our being called children of light, our sharing in eternal glory, and, in a word, our being brought into a state of all *fulness of blessing*, both in this world and in the world to come, of all the good gifts that are in store for us, by promise hereof, through faith, beholding the reflection of their grace as though they were already present, we await the full enjoyment." - St. Basil

The Descent of the Holy Spirit

"O Holy Spirit, descend plentifully into my heart. Enlighten the dark corners of this neglected dwelling and scatter there Thy cheerful beams." - St. Augustine

Rosary Meditations

The Fourth Glorious Mystery: The Assumption of the Blessed Virgin Mary

Scripture References

Genesis 3:15; Luke 1:28; Revelation 12:1-6

The Story in Brief

Mary remained on earth for several years after her Son ascended into Heaven. At the end of her natural life, she was taken, body and soul, into Heaven to live in eternal joy with the Blessed Trinity.

Points to Ponder

1. Although the Assumption of Mary into Heaven is not explicitly mentioned in the Scriptures, the Church's Sacred Tradition has held for centuries that Mary was assumed into Heaven, body and soul, at the end of her natural life. Reflect on the relationship between Scripture and Tradition. Think about how Tradition gave rise to Scripture and how the seeds planted in Scripture bloom in Tradition.

2. Mary's Assumption flows from her Immaculate Conception. If death and bodily corruption occur because

Rosary Meditations

of sin, then the sinless one, Mary, would not be constrained by such things. Meditate on the wonderful fact that Mary was conceived without sin and remained sinless her entire life.

3. Read Genesis 3, paying special attention to Genesis 3:15. This verse is often called the Protoevangelium, or first Gospel, for it promises a Redeemer born of a woman. Ponder how this verse predicts and describes Mary and Jesus. Focus especially on the word "enmity," which refers to a complete antagonism between the woman and the serpent and between the woman's offspring and the serpent's offspring.[52] How does this enmity support the dogma of Mary's sinlessness?

4. In Luke 1:28, the archangel Gabriel called Mary "full of grace." A literal translation from the Greek is "the one having been filled with grace."[53] Meditate on Mary's fullness of grace.

5. Read Revelation 12:1-6. How do these verses describe Mary?

6. Even though Mary was sinless, she still relied on Jesus for her salvation. Theologians explain that the merits Jesus Christ would win on the cross were applied to Mary beforehand in a form of preservative redemption. She was thereby preserved from sin.[54] Meditate on these truths.

7. Why was it so important for Jesus to be born of a sinless mother?

8. Why did Mary remain on earth for many years after Jesus ascended into Heaven? What was her role in the

The Assumption

early Church? Ponder the suffering Mary must have experienced when she was separated from her Son.

9. No one knows for sure whether Mary actually died at the end of her life or whether she was assumed into Heaven without tasting death. The Eastern Church speaks of Mary's dormition (i.e., her transition to eternal life through a kind of sleep) while the Western Church leans toward the conclusion that Mary, in imitation of her Son, did actually die. Contemplate these ideas. Which seems more likely to you?

10. A pious legend that has come down to us from the early years of the Church describes the end of Mary's life. All the apostles except Thomas had gathered around Mary's deathbed to say goodbye. Reflect on the relationship between the apostles and Mary and on the apostles' sadness at losing her.

11. According to the legend, Thomas arrived after Mary had been laid in her tomb. He wanted to see her one last time and went to the tomb to look at the woman who had become his mother. When the tomb was opened, Thomas found a multitude of fragrant flowers, roses and lilies, but Mary's body was gone. Picture the scene and Thomas' reaction.

12. Imagine Mary's arrival in Heaven and her joyous reunion with her Son.

13. Except for Jesus, Mary is the only being in Heaven who has both a body and a soul. Reflect on the significance of this. How does Mary's Assumption foreshadow the general resurrection at the end of time?

Rosary Meditations

14. Meditate on Mary's great love for God and His people.

15. Spend some time meditating on one or more artistic image of the Assumption.[55] How does each image present the event? How does it depict Mary?

Application Questions

1. How do you view the relationship between Sacred Scripture and Sacred Tradition? Do you fully understand and appreciate the rich Tradition of the Catholic Church? How might you grow in your knowledge and appreciation?

2. Do you have a strong relationship with Mary? Is she your mother? Why or why not? How might you strengthen your relationship with Mary?

3. In which areas of your life do you need to repent? Which sins are most challenging for you? How might you claim Mary's help in overcoming your sins?

4. Has death ever separated you from a loved one? How does that feel? How do you cope?

5. Are you looking forward to happy reunions with those who have already passed over into eternal life? Can you imagine what those reunions might be like?

6. How do you express your longing for eternal life with God in Heaven?

7. Do you imitate Mary in your love for God and other people? How might you do so more often and to a greater extent?

The Assumption

Prayer, Prayer, and More Prayer

Blessing and Adoration – Father, Son, and Holy Spirit, we bow down before You in silent adoration as we contemplate the great graces You have given Mary and as we meditate on her Assumption into Heaven. We bless You for the wonders of Mary, for she magnifies You.

Praise – Jesus, we praise You for Your saving power. We praise You for applying that power to Your mother at the moment of her conception that she might be a sinless vessel fit to bear You, her God and her Son. We praise You for assuming Your mother, body and soul, into Heaven that she may stand as a sign of hope for all of us who await the fullness of eternal life.

Thanksgiving – Jesus, thank You for Mary, Your mother and our mother. Thank You for her sinlessness that shows us how to love and her Assumption that gives us reason to hope that we, too, will one day be with You in Heaven, body and soul.

Intercession – Jesus, we lift up to You all Christians who do not have a relationship with Mary. We lift up those who do not understand or believe that she is their mother who loves them and prays for them. Introduce them to Mary, Lord, that they may know and love her.

Petition – Holy Trinity, we pray that we may follow Mary more closely. We pray that we may love as she did, open our hearts to You as she did, and surrender ourselves to You as she did. We pray that someday we may be with You and Mother Mary forever in Heaven.

Rosary Meditations

Quotes from the Saints and Popes

"The course of this life having been completed by blessed Mary, when now she would be called from the world, all the apostles came together from their various regions to her house. And when they had heard that she was about to be taken from the world, they kept watch together with her. And behold, the Lord Jesus came with His angels, and, taking her soul, He gave it over to the angel Michael and withdrew. At daybreak, however, the apostles took up her body on a bier and placed it in a tomb, and they guarded it, expecting the Lord to come. And behold, again the Lord stood by them; the holy body having been received, He commanded that it be taken in a cloud into paradise, where now, rejoined to the soul, [Mary's body] rejoices with the Lord's chosen ones and is in the enjoyment of the good of an eternity that will never end."
- St. Gregory of Tours[56]

"The Assumption is the culmination of the struggle which involved Mary's generous love in the redemption of humanity and is the fruit of her unique sharing in the victory of the Cross." - Blessed John Paul II[57]

"It was fitting that she, who had kept her virginity intact in childbirth, should keep her own body free from all corruption even after death. It was fitting that she, who had carried the Creator as a child at her breast, should dwell in the divine tabernacles. It was fitting that the spouse, whom the Father had taken to Himself, should live in the divine mansions. It was fitting that she, who had seen her Son upon the cross and who had thereby received into her heart the sword of sorrow which she had escaped in the act of giving birth to Him, should look upon Him as He sits with the Father. It was fitting that

The Assumption

God's Mother should possess what belongs to her Son, and that she should be honored by every creature as the Mother and as the handmaid of God." - St. John Damascene[58]

"You are she who, as it is written, appears in beauty, and your virginal body is all holy, all chaste, entirely the dwelling place of God, so that it is henceforth completely exempt from dissolution into dust. Though still human, it is changed into the heavenly life of incorruptibility, truly living and glorious, undamaged and sharing in perfect life." - St. Germanus of Constantinople[59]

"As the most glorious Mother of Christ, our Savior and God and the giver of life and immortality, has been endowed with life by Him, she has received an eternal incorruptibility of the body together with Him Who has raised her up from the tomb and has taken her up to Himself in a way known only to Him." - St. Modestus of Jerusalem[60]

"For which reason, after we have poured forth prayers of supplication again and again to God, and have invoked the light of the Spirit of Truth, for the glory of Almighty God Who has lavished His special affection upon the Virgin Mary, for the honor of her Son, the immortal King of the Ages and the Victor over sin and death, for the increase of the glory of that same august Mother, and for the joy and exultation of the entire Church; by the authority of our Lord Jesus Christ, of the Blessed Apostles Peter and Paul, and by our own authority, we pronounce, declare, and define it to be a divinely revealed dogma: that the Immaculate Mother of God, the ever Virgin Mary, having completed the course of her earthly life, was assumed body and soul into heavenly glory." - Pope Pius XII[61]

The Fifth Glorious Mystery: The Coronation of the Blessed Virgin Mary

Scripture References

John 2:1-12; Revelation 12:1

The Story in Brief

After Mary was assumed, body and soul, into Heaven, the Blessed Trinity, with great love, crowned her as Queen of Heaven and Earth. Under this title, Mary acts as Queen Mother, Advocate, and Mediatrix to the human family.

Points to Ponder

1. After being assumed, body and soul, into Heaven, Mary was crowned Queen of Heaven and Earth by the Blessed Trinity. We catch a glimpse of Mary as queen in Revelation 12:1. Picture Mary in the splendor of her queenship.

2. Mary stands as the Queen Mother. In the ancient world, it was common for the king's mother to hold the position of queen in the royal household. The queen filled the roles of advocate for the people and mediatrix

between the king and his subjects.[62] Reflect on Mary as the Queen Mother.

3. Mary serves as an Advocate, interceding with her Son for the needs and longings of the human race. Ponder Mary's intercession.

4. Saints and theologians have often taught that all graces come from God to humanity through Mary. They call Mary the "Mediatrix of All Graces" and explain that Jesus has given His mother the right to nourish all her children with grace.[63] Ponder Mary's role as Mediatrix of All Graces.

5. Read the story of the wedding at Cana in John 2:1-12. What did Mary do at Cana? Why did she do so? What did she say? How did her Son respond? How do Mary's words and actions at Cana illustrate her queenship and her roles as Advocate and Mediatrix?

6. Mary is the queen because she is the mother of Jesus, the divine Son of God. Reflect on Mary's loving, intimate, maternal relationship with her Son.

7. Mary is also our mother. Reflect on Mary's loving, intimate, maternal relationship with her human children.

8. We owe obedience and honor to our queen and mother. Think about the special veneration, not worship, that we Catholics show toward Mary.

9. Even though Mary is very close to us, she also reigns in supreme dignity. Pope Pius IX explains, God "showered her with heavenly gifts and graces from the treasury of His divinity so far beyond what He gave to all the angels

The Coronation

and saints that she was ever free from the least stain of sin; she is so beautiful and perfect, and possesses such fullness of innocence and holiness, that under God a greater could not be dreamed, and only God can comprehend the marvel."[64] Reflect on these beautiful words.

10. Pray the Litany of the Blessed Virgin Mary before beginning the Rosary.[65] Ponder each of Mary's titles.

11. Meditate on various images of Mary as Queen of Heaven and Earth.[66] How do these images portray Mary? What kinds of symbolism do they use?

12. Read about some modern Marian apparitions like Lourdes, Fatima, and Medjugorje.[67] Why does Mary appear to some of her children? What messages does she bring?

Application Questions

1. What kind of relationship do you have with Mary? How important is she in your spiritual life?

2. In what circumstances has Mary acted as your Advocate? How often do you ask Mary to intercede for you?

3. What are your deepest needs and longings? Do you take them to your mother Mary and ask for her help? Why or why not?

4. Have you ever turned to Mary as Mediatrix to receive a special grace? Why or why not? Do you understand that

the graces you receive from God come through Mary? What do you think of this?

5. How is Mary your mother? How do you respond to her motherly love?

6. How do you venerate Mary? How do you explain your veneration of Mary to others who question or criticize it?

7. Which of Mary's titles resonates most with you? Why?

8. What is your opinion of Marian apparitions? Which apparition or message especially speaks to your heart?

Prayer, Prayer, and More Prayer

Blessing and Adoration – Blessed Trinity, we bow before You in silent adoration as we gaze with eyes of faith upon Mary, our mother and queen. We bless You for the great blessings You have poured out upon her, and we adore You as we venerate her.

Praise – We praise You, Jesus, for loving us so much that You have made Your mother our mother. We praise You for designating her as our queen, Advocate, and Mediatrix. We praise You as we sing her praises.

Thanksgiving – Thank You, Lord, for Mary. Thank You for sending her to us in apparitions all over the world. Thank You for her messages, her guidance, and her love, which communicate Your messages, Your guidance, and Your love.

Intercession – Lord, we lift up to You all Christians who do not have a devotion to Mary. We lift up those who do

The Coronation

not believe that she is their queen, mother, Advocate, and Mediatrix. We lift up those who scoff at Mary and say that she was "just the mother" and no more. Introduce them to Your mother, Lord, so that they may see how much she loves them, nourishes them, and prays for them.

Petition – Lord, help us to grow ever closer to Mary. Inspire us to turn to her for love, assistance, guidance, and motherly care. Help us to love Your mother as You love her.

<u>Quotes from the Saints</u>

"Such is the will of God that we should have everything through Mary." - St. Alphonsus Liguori[68]

"But the power of Mary over all the devils will especially shine forth in the latter times, when Satan will lay his snares against her heel: that is to say, her humble slaves and her poor children, whom she will raise up to make war against him. They shall be little and poor in the world's esteem, and abased before all like the heel, trodden underfoot and persecuted as the heel is by the other members of the body. But in return for this they shall be rich in the grace of God, which Mary shall distribute to them abundantly. They shall be great and exalted before God in sanctity, superior to all other creatures by their lively zeal, and so well sustained with God's assistance that, with the humility of their heel, in union with Mary, they shall crush the head of the devil and cause Jesus Christ to triumph." - St. Louis de Montfort[69]

Rosary Meditations

"Mary is the sure path to our meeting with Christ. Devotion to the Mother of the Lord, when it is genuine, is always an impetus to a life guided by the spirit and values of the Gospel." - Blessed John Paul II[70]

"As mariners are guided into port by the shining of a star, so Christians are guided to heaven by Mary." - St. Thomas Aquinas[71]

"To give worthy praise to the Lord's mercy, we unite ourselves with Your Immaculate Mother, for then our hymn will be more pleasing to You, because She is chosen from among men and angels. Through Her, as through a pure crystal, Your mercy was passed on to us. Through Her, man became pleasing to God; through Her, streams of grace flowed down upon us." - St. Faustina[72]

"Never be afraid of loving the Blessed Virgin too much. You can never love her more than Jesus did." - St. Maximilian Kolbe[73]

"In dangers, in doubts, in difficulties, think of Mary, call upon Mary. Let not her name depart from your lips, never suffer it to leave your heart. And that you may obtain the assistance of her prayer, neglect not to walk in her footsteps. With her for guide, you shall never go astray; while invoking her, you shall never lose heart; so long as she is in your mind, you are safe from deception; while she holds your hand, you cannot fall; under her protection you have nothing to fear; if she walks before you, you shall not grow weary; if she shows you favor, you shall reach the goal." - St. Bernard of Clairvaux[74]

The Coronation

"Let us run to Mary, and, as her little children, cast ourselves into her arms with a perfect confidence." - St. Francis de Sales[75]

"In trial or difficulty I have recourse to Mother Mary, whose glance alone is enough to dissipate every fear." - St. Thérèse of Lisieux[76]

"Mary has the authority over the angels and the blessed in Heaven. As a reward for her great humility, God gave her the power and mission of assigning to saints the thrones made vacant by the apostate angels who fell away through pride. Such is the will of the almighty God Who exalts the humble, that the powers of Heaven, earth and hell, willingly or unwillingly, must obey the commands of the humble Virgin Mary. For God has made her Queen of Heaven and Earth, leader of His armies, keeper of His treasure, dispenser of His graces, Mediatrix on behalf of men, destroyer of His enemies, and faithful associate in His great works and triumphs." - St. Louis de Montfort[77]

Rosary Meditations

Notes

[1] "Nazareth," *Wikipedia*, http://en.wikipedia.org/wiki/Nazareth (accessed August 16, 2013.

[2] John A. Hardon, *Pocket Catholic Dictionary* (New York: Doubleday, 1985), 342.

[3] Unless otherwise noted, quotations from the saints are taken from St. Thomas Aquinas' *Catena Aurea*. The full text of *Catena Aurea* is available online at several websites, including Christian Classics Ethereal Library (www.ccel.org) and Internet Archive (archive.org).

[4] Great Treasures, http://greattreasures.org (accessed October 13, 2012). Whenever Greek words are noted and defined in the text, the definitions come from this website.

[5] Ibid.

[6] Ibid.

[7] Kevin Orlin Johnson, *Rosary: Mysteries, Meditations, and the Telling of the Beads* (Dallas: Pangaeus Press, 2002), 258.

[8] Wayne Blank, "The Jordon River," *Daily Bible Study*, http://www.keyway.ca/htm2000/20000406.htm (accessed September 2, 2013).

[9] Great Treasures.

[10] *The Navarre Bible: St. Matthew* (Dublin: Four Courts Press, 2003), 40.

[11] Great Treasures.

[12] Ibid.

[13] Pope Benedict XVI, *Jesus of Nazareth: From the Baptism in the Jordan to the Transfiguration* (San Francisco: Ignatius Press, 2007), 9-24.

[14] For more information about Mary as Co-redemptrix, Mediatrix, and Advocate, see Mark Miravalle's *Introduction to Mary: The Heart of Marian Doctrine and Devotion* (Goleta, CA: Queenship, 1993).

[15] Nicholas Hardesty, "Catholic Q&A #10: Did Jesus rebuke Mary at the wedding feast at Cana?", Owensboro Catholic Radio, http://owensborocatholicradio.com/622/catholic-qa-10-did-jesus-rebuke-mary-at-the-wedding-feast-at-cana/ (accessed October 22, 2012).

[16] The full text of *Catena Aurea* is available online at several websites, including Christian Classics Ethereal Library (www.ccel.org) and Internet Archive (archive.org).

[17] See, for example, Eric Lyons' article "Six or Eight Days?" at Apologetics Press (http://www.apologeticspress.org/apcontent.aspx?category=6&article=757).

[18] See, for example, the tract on "Creation and Genesis" at Catholic Answers (http://www.catholic.com/tracts/creation-and-genesis) and the *Catechism of the Catholic Church* #1274.

[19] Great Treasures.

[20] Ibid.

[21] See, for example, Jimmy Akin's article "10 Things You Need to Know about Jesus' Transfiguration" at http://www.ncregister.com/blog/jimmy-akin/10-things-you-need-to-know-about-jesus-transfiguration.

[22] Scott Hahn's article "The Hunt for the Fourth Cup" is available online at http://archive.catholic.com/thisrock/1991/9109fea1.asp.

[23] Great Treasures.

Notes

[24] In-depth teaching on the Eucharist may be found in #1322-#1419 of the *Catechism of the Catholic Church*, which is available online at the Vatican website (http://www.vatican.va/archive/ENG0015/_INDEX.HTM) or the United States Conference of Catholic Bishops website (http://www.usccb.org/beliefs-and-teachings/what-we-believe/catechism/catechism-of-the-catholic-church/) as well as in print form.

[25] Visit the Real Presence Eucharistic Education and Adoration Association online at http://www.therealpresence.org/. Click on the monstrance on the homepage to access in-depth information about the Eucharist.

[26] Also at the Real Presence Eucharistic Education and Adoration Association (http://www.therealpresence.org/), click on the "Testimonies" button for dozens of quotes from the saints.

[27] "Gethsemane," *Bible Study Tools*, http://www.biblestudytools.com/dictionary/gethsemane/ (accessed December 3, 2013).

[28] Great Treasures.

[29] Ibid.

[30] See, for example, Anne Catherine Emmerich's *The Dolorous Passion of Our Lord Jesus Christ*, Part III, Chapter I.

[31] Great Treasures.

[32] Ibid.; see, for example, Anne Catherine Emmerich's *The Dolorous Passion of Our Lord Jesus Christ*, Part III, Chapter I.

[33] "Scourging," The Crucifixion, http://the-crucifixion.org/scourging.htm (accessed November 5, 2012).

[34] For more information, see Eric Lyons' article "Was the Robe Placed on Jesus Scarlet or Purple" at http://www.apologeticspress.org/apcontent.aspx?category=6&article=300.

[35] Johnson, 279-281.

[36] Versions of the Stations of the Cross are available online at EWTN (http://www.ewtn.com/devotionals/stations/face.htm); Creighton University (http://onlineministries.creighton.edu/CollaborativeMinistry/stations.html); and Catholic Online (http://www.catholic.org/clife/prayers/ station.php).

[37] Scott Hahn, *A Father Who Keeps His Promises* (Cincinnati: Servant Books, 1998), 109.

[38] Albert Barnes, "Matthew 27:34," *Notes on the Bible*, e-Sword Bible software.

[39] Great Treasures.

[40] Scott Hahn's article "The Hunt for the Fourth Cup" is available online at http://archive.catholic.com/thisrock/1991/9109fea1.asp.

[41] See, for example, "Holy Saturday: He Descended into Hell" at http://www.crossroadsinitiative.com/library_article/380/Holy_Saturday____He_Descended_Into_Hell.html (accessed December 3, 2013).

[42] See, for example, *The Catechism of the Catholic Church* #2174.

[43] Harmonizations may be found at New Advent (http://www.newadvent.org/cathen/12789a.htm) and Tekton (http://www.tektonics.org/harmonize/greenharmony.htm).

[44] Great Treasures.

[45] John Henry Newman, *Parochial and Plain Sermons*, Vol. 6 (London: Scribner, Welford, &Co., 1868), 231.

[46] Thomas Aquinas, *Summa Theologica*, III, Q57, Art 6 (London: R. & T. Washbourne, Ltd., 1914), 438.

Notes

[47] For more information about Pentecost, see New Advent (http://www.newadvent.org/cathen/11661a.htm and http://www.newadvent.org/cathen/15614b.htm); Catholic Online (http://www.catholic.org/clife/lent/pentecost.php); and *Navarre Study Bible: Acts* (Dublin: Four Courts Press, 2003), 30-33.
[48] Great Treasures.
[49] Ibid.
[50] EWTN's pages on the Holy Spirit are available at http://www.ewtn.com/faith/teachings/spirmenu.htm.
[51] Fr. William Saunders' article on the gifts of the Holy Spirit is available at http://www.catholiceducation.org/articles/religion/re0451.html.
[52] Mark Miravalle, *Introduction to Mary: The Heart of Marian Doctrine and Devotion* (Goleta, CA: Queenship, 1993), 24.
[53] Ibid., 66.
[54] Ibid., 71-72.
[55] To access images of the Assumption, type "Assumption" into the Google Images search box.
[56] "Mary: 'Full of Grace,'" *Catholic Answers*, http://www.catholic.com/tracts/mary-full-of-grace (accessed December 24, 2012).
[57] John Paul II, "Church Believes in Mary's Assumption," *Vatican*, http://www.vatican.va/holy_father/john_paul_ii/audiences/1997/documents/hf_jp-ii_aud_02071997_en.html (accessed November 7, 2013).
[58] Pius XII, "Munificentissimus Deus," *Vatican*, http://www.vatican.va/holy_father/pius_xii/apost_constitutions/documents/hf_pxii_apc_19501101_munificentissimus-deus_en.html (accessed December 24, 2012).
[59] Ibid.
[60] Ibid.
[61] Ibid.

[62] Michal Hunt, "The Blessed Virgin Mary: Queen Mother of the New Davidic Kingdom," *Agape Bible Study*, 2006, http://www.agapebiblestudy.com/documents/mary%20the%20queen%20mother%20of%20the%20new%20davidic%20kingdom.htm (accessed November 7, 2013).

[63] See Miravalle, 88-94.

[64] Pius XII, "Ad Caeli Reginam," *Vatican*, http://www.vatican.va/holy_father/pius_xii/encyclicals/documents/hf_p-xii_enc_11101954_ad-caeli-reginam_en.html (accessed November 7, 2013).

[65] The Litany of the Blessed Virgin Mary is available online at http://campus.udayton.edu/mary/prayers/bvm.html.

[66] To access images of the queenship of Mary type "Queenship of Mary" into the Google Images search box.

[67] For more information about Lourdes, visit http://www.marypages.com/bernadetteEng1.htm. For more information about Fatima, visit http://www.ewtn.com/fatima/. For more information about Medjugorje, visit www.medjugorje.org.

[68] "Mary's Page Quotes," *Gardenias 4 Lina*, http://www.gardenias4lina.com/mary_page_quotes.html (accessed December 24, 2012).

[69] Ibid.

[70] Ibid.

[71] "Our Lady, Star of the Sea: 10 Quotes About the Blessed Virgin," *St. Peter's List*, http://www.stpeterslist.com/1025/our-lady-star-of-the-sea-10-quotes-about-the-blessed-virgin/ (accessed December 24, 2012).

[72] Maria Faustina Kowalska, *Diary: Divine Mercy in My Soul* (Stockbridge, MA: Marians of the Immaculate Conception, 1987), 618.

[73] "On the Blessed Virgin Mary...," *Catholic Quotations*, http://catholicquotations.blogspot.com/2007/12/necessity-of-devotion-to-blessed-virgin.html (accessed December 24, 2012).

[74] "Our Lady, Star of the Sea."

[75] Ibid.

[76] "Mary, mother of God," White Lily of Trinity, http://whitelilyoftrinity.com/saints_quotes_mary.html (accessed December 24, 2012).

[77] "On the Blessed Virgin Mary...."

CPSIA information can be obtained
at www.ICGtesting.com
Printed in the USA
LVOW13s1126301017
554256LV00046B/1248/P